"THE DUCHESS OF MARISTER WAS CONDUCTED TO THE SCARLET ROOM AND STOOD GAZING AT THE PICTURE CALLED 'THE HAUNTED PAGODA'"

THE INTERNATIONAL ADVENTURE LIBRARY

THREE OWLS EDITION

THE RADIUM TERRORS

A Mystery Story

BY

ALBERT DORRINGTON

WILDSIDE PRESS

THE RADIUM TERRORS

THE RADIUM TERRORS

CHAPTER I

I'VE been hunting for a little god
that escaped from some pitchblende,
Tony!" Gifford Renwick entered the
smoking room of the International Inquiry
Bureau shaking the raindrops from his hat
and coat.

Tony Hackett, a small, cherubic man with
wheat-red hair and uncertain eyes, was seated
near the fire. Renwick's words caused a
listening blindness to cloud his glance. He
responded without looking up at the young
man beside him.

"If I were to hazard a guess, Renwick,"
he said thoughtfully, "I should say that
your god will hate you like poison when
you've found him. Sit down and let's
hear."

Renwick's boyish face was flushed from the
effects of some recent excitement; a nervous
expectancy strained him to the point of
laughter.

"I've been smoke-hunting," he declared

with an effort, "in the hope of finding a genius tucked away in the coils."

"Well!"

Renwick shrugged. "I came very near to making an ass of myself, Tony — the same old donkey that brays on the slightest provocation."

"You are the only youngster in Coleman's service who can differentiate between an astral body and an Army mule," Hackett admitted graciously. "You've been chasing those radium thieves, I suppose," he added. "Don't let 'em worry you, Renny. The god in the pitchblende is going to whiten the hair of your superiors before the case is over. Try golf with your whiskey for a change. It's wonderfully soothing."

Gifford Renwick dropped into the big armchair to study the gray smoke and reddening flames, for he had found the key of many a teasing problem hidden in the white ashes of a winter fire.

The room in which they sat was one set apart by Anthony Coleman for the use of his officials. Gifford Renwick had become a member of Coleman's private detective service some three years before. The salary paid him was infinitesimal, the prospects of increased pay enormous. Tony Hackett had reached the three-hundred-a-year line, while Renwick, in his twenty-third year, did official spadework for half the amount.

The theft of the Moritz radium tube had quickened his senses. For the first time in life he was brought within the operation area of an unknown criminal organization, and the experience made him feel humble and ashamed.

A glass tube containing six grains of pure radium, valued at as many thousand pounds, had been stolen from the laboratory of Prof. Eugene Moritz. At Scotland Yard the affair was diagnosed as a bit of "ghost work," without parallel in the annals of unsolved mysteries.

To Renwick the case presented itself as the most fascinating problem in modern criminology. Professor Moritz averred that the radium tube had disappeared while he was engaged in conversation at the laboratory telephone.

At the time of the incident, the professor deposed, the doors and windows of the laboratory were securely fastened. There had been no possible way of entry without his knowledge. About eleven o'clock in the morning he had received a call at the telephone. Placing the glass tube containing the radium on his work-table, he had turned aside for a few moments to take hold of the receiver. When he returned to the table the tube was missing.

Previously to the incident he had been engaged in a series of experiments which, according to custom, had been conducted with windows and doors locked to prevent unlooked-for interruptions. Professor Moritz was emphatic in his statements that no living person could have entered the laboratory unknown to him. The members of his household were never permitted to interrupt him while certain experiments were in progress.

One Scotland Yard official suggested that the radium tube had probably found its way into the heated crucible, and had become absorbed in the molten mass of mineral substances contained therein. The contents of the crucible had therefore been subjected to a searching analysis without revealing the slightest trace of any radio-active matter.

Gifford Renwick had preferred to let the

case rest until it was relegated to the official pigeon-holes to await, with the other forgotten mysteries, the resurrecting trumpet of some unborn genius. In the interest of his employer Renwick had entered upon a series of investigations which, in his estimation, had been left uncovered by the Scotland Yard experts.

What manner of thief, he asked himself, could effect an entrance into a locked laboratory at a time when a very astute scientist was himself the only occupant?

The laboratory was situated at the rear of Professor Moritz's house, and was in no way connected with the main building. The floor was of smooth concrete and free from crevices. There was no possible way of entry by the roof even if Moritz had been absent from the laboratory at the time of the occurrence.

In the adjoining house lived a Japanese doctor, Teroni Tsarka by name, whose fame as a nerve specialist had brought him into public notice.

Renwick had paid some attention to the movements of the Japanese doctor, with uninspiring results. There was little to be learned by casually watching a small, shrivelled Asiatic who rarely ventured out of doors unless in a fast-moving car which allowed no time for personal criticisms or interrogations.

Doctor Tsarka had one daughter, Pepio, a laughing, mischievous girl of eighteen, who ventured abroad with the audacity of an American heiress. Father and daughter had been in England about a year; both were linguists of exceptional ability. It was Pepio's elusiveness which had pointed the young detective's interest in them. Always unapproachable and studiously alert, the laughing-eyed Pepio was usually accompanied by a youth of her own nationality whose name, he learned afterward, was Soto Inouyiti. Like Doctor Tsarka, Soto Inouyiti had attracted public attention by his collection of pictures exhibited some months before at his rooms in South Kensington.

Renwick had shadowed the pair during their daily excursions through the city, only to discover that the love of art and literature was their besetting sin. Soto was scarcely eighteen; a slim, pretty boy with an oval face and skin of a peculiar olive richness.

Their innocent love of pictures and English books was a discovery that in no way coincided with Renwick's idea of Doctor Tsarka's complicity in the Moritz radium mystery. So he relinquished them with a sigh, and on the very day he abandoned his Tsarka theory he met Pepio on the stairs of a reference library in St. Martin's Place.

The stairway was badly lit, and his eye was transfixed by a luminescent ray emitted from a peculiar metal brooch that held Pepio's silk shawl to her shoulders. She passed him very swiftly, and was gone before his mind had leaped back to the main trail.

So he had returned to the office to brood upon the peculiar light emissions which appeared to radiate from the throat ornaments worn by Tsarka's laughing-eyed daughter. What manner of gem was it that could illuminate the darkness of a stairway? he pondered.

Tony Hackett laughed at his prolonged silence, and then very suddenly found himself staring into Renwick's handsome face.

"By jove, Gif, I really think you have dropped on to something," he broke out. "The last time I saw you so misty about the eyes was when you had the Wilmot boy in your grip — the little wretch!"

Renwick looked annoyed, and the shadow on his brow brought an instant apology from the good-natured Tony.

"I blame you for allowing the young imp to slip away, though," he added, feeling that it was not good to apologize without a shot in another direction.

Gifford's softness of heart was well known among his intimates. It was a fact which had also been noted by various members of the criminal classes, who used their knowledge with craft and circumspection whenever his sympathies were attracted in any given direction.

The Wilmot affair was a case in point. Employed by a firm of warehousemen at an exceedingly low wage, young Wilmot had been drawn by an older clerk into a system of petty pilferings which amounted to nearly a hundred pounds. Wilmot's family were in straitened circumstances, and the boy's borrowings had gone to relieve the sickness and distress which had come upon them through the unexpected death of the father. At the last moment Renwick had neglected to insure the boy's arrest, and Oliver Wilmot had escaped to America, where he was soon in a position to refund in full the amount of his defalcations.

Renwick's act in allowing the boy to elude his employers at the last moment had nearly caused his own dismissal from the service of Anthony Coleman. He escaped, however, with a severe lecture on the sin of aiding young and foolish persons to evade the law's just penalty.

Tony Hackett's words scarcely roused Gifford from his brooding quiet. When he spoke the dream glow of the red fire was in his eyes.

"I've been walking all day," he said without looking up, "tramp, tramp, tramping in the wake of lost ideas until —— "

He paused almost sharply as though conscious of his companion's searching glances.

"Until what?" Tony demanded bluntly. "Say on, Renny. Don't stew in your own dream palaces too long."

Gifford was silent for a period of six heartbeats. Then his voice had the weary intonation of an awakened sleeper.

"I met a young lady to-day who has

been evading my attentions for some time. I'd fixed on her father as the kind of man likely to have been mixed up in the Moritz case. I've lived near the hem of her shadow for a long time until I was satisfied that she or her people were not the kind I was after. I came upon her to-day on the stairs of a reference library, a pretty darkish place, and I discovered that she was in a highly radio-active condition!"

Tony was not scientifically disposed, and his companion's words fell a trifle short of their true significance. Gifford explained.

"The young lady I refer to has been at close quarters with a quantity of chemical matter, in a laboratory perhaps, and it may have happened that she has been allowed to handle radium carelessly."

"Is this radio-activity easily detected in persons?"

"Yes; it acts like phosphorus in the dark. It may get on the fingers, and, as a matter of course, to the metal trinkets or jewellery worn by the experimenter or thief. It was the young lady's brooch flaring in the dark that caught me."

Tony sighed. "A lot depends whether she

or her people have been handling the Moritz radium. If you first suspected her of the theft, and then discovered a radium flare on her person, your inductions are pretty sound. Personally I'd have shadowed her to the skyline on the strength of your clue."

He stared at the brooding boyish face in amazement. "If she's pretty you'll let her go, Renny. But take an old stager's advice and get your friend McFee, of Scotland Yard, to shoot her into clink to-night. It's the chance of a lifetime; it's fame with a big F. Why "— he paused to hammer Renwick's stooping shoulders with his fist — "this Moritz radium case fairly smothered the Scotland Yard people; it created a vacancy in their thinking department and gave their best men a pain in the neck through waiting round corners. Gifford, my boy, don't let this radio-active girl slip through your fingers."

"It will be like arresting a Madonna," Gifford confessed. "I shall have to get it done though."

"When you grow older you'll be less merciful to thieves and scoundrels," Hackett averred. "So get McFee on the Madonna's trail without delay. It will do you a lot of good with the firm after your —— "

"Recent bunglings, eh?"

"Well, yes, Gif. Lately you've allowed a lot of good things to slip past. Lay to your clue and keep your intellect bright."

Gifford sighed as he prepared to depart. "I like theory work best. When it comes to 'putting away' old men and — and children it makes one feel rather lonesome — cowardly almost. Good-night, Tony!"

For a while Renwick deliberated on the wisdom of bringing his friend McFee into his scheme of things. Professor Moritz had come for help to the International Inquiry Bureau, feeling assured that Scotland Yard was treating his story as the result of an overwrought imagination. He desired nothing more than the return of his lost radium. He was the type of man who abhorred criminal prosecutions and the air of police courts.

Therefore, Renwick argued, if it were possible to gain admission into the Japanese doctor's house, he might succeed, after hinting delicately at police intervention and exposure, in recovering the lost radium bulb.

The bluff had worked before. If McFee were introduced, anything might happen. The Scotland Yard man would naturally make the most of his chance. There would be a sudden rush into the house of the Japanese doctor; much noise and tramping of feet — circumstances likely to permit one of Tsarka's people to escape with the precious *cache* of radium.

In a fraction of time Renwick decided to act on his own responsibility. If trouble arose he might easily communicate with McFee and bring about the Jap's arrest. On the other hand, if his bluff succeeded the radium could be returned to Moritz and things left to take their course. Only he prayed inwardly that the Madonna-faced Pepio would never fall foul of his friend McFee. The big Scotch detective had a freckled skin and the spring of a tiger. No . . . it would not be good for Pepio San.

Renwick felt the rain sting his cheek as he passed into the street. The lamps shone moon-white through the uprising mists. Shapes flitted past with almost ghostly stealth, while here and there he saw half-dressed waifs crouching in office doorways, baby-like children muffled in rags, the hunger-wolf alive in their wind-purpled faces.

The entrance to Doctor Tsarka's house was lit by a pair of pedestal lamps. A well-kept lawn with a thickset hedge separated it from the road. Gifford had mapped out no particular plan of action, but trusted that some propitious circumstance would enable him to enter the Japanese doctor's house as swiftly as possible. To go in as a patient with a view to a consultation seemed the only way. A moment's reflection, however, revealed the folly of such a proceeding.

Stooping in the shadow of the hedge he waited while the passing minutes lengthened into eternities. The theatre cars sped past in a rapid procession. A glance at his watch showed him that it was past eleven. Pausing near the gate entrance he observed a small Daimler landaulette halt suddenly within a few yards of the pavement. Pepio Tsarka slipped out and passed through the gate before he had recovered from his surprise.

At the first touch of the house bell the door opened smartly to allow her a swift entry. Renwick almost leaped on her heels as she passed in, his shoulder hurling back the door in the face of a slant-eyed Japanese servant.

Pepio faced him instantly, the quick blood darkening her olive cheek. "How dare you come in here!" she flashed. "What is your business?"

"Your excellent parent, Pepio San." He was breathing hard like one who had gained the threshold of a long-desired goal. "A question of his naturalization papers. I would like to see them."

She stamped her foot. "You have no right of entry here. Our Consul shall hear of it!"

Gifford had been loth to force his way into the house of Doctor Tsarka. Yet a hurried glance at the palpitating Japanese girl convinced him that his visit was not wholly unexpected.

Retreating with the servant along the wide entrance hall she stayed in the shadow of a portière, her eyes turned in his direction. He was again conscious of the peculiar light emissions which surrounded her.

"Are you aware, Miss Tsarka, that you are radio-active?" He smiled reassuringly while his left hand closed the house door softly.

She retreated farther, her fingers straying

instinctively over the tell-tale brooch. Renwick experienced an unexpected thrill at the strange silence of the house, a silence that closed around him with the solidity of a bank vault. Her voice reached him, but this time he detected a certain malicious merriment in it.

"My father receives visits from many hopeless lunatics. Probably you are the victim of overwork?" she queried.

Her dark, mischievous eyes seemed to reflect the luminescent flow of light from her dress ornaments. Before Gifford could reply a door opened noiselessly at the passage end. He found himself examining a shadowy, bull-necked little man with Japanese eyes and close-cropped head.

He looked once at Pepio and then at the young detective. "You make great intrusion here," he growled. "Say, what heart trouble sends you so late? Doctor Tsarka is indisposed!"

Renwick felt that he had allowed the brooch incident to betray him. His mind leaped to the double as he glanced from Pepio to the scowling Jap, half concealed in the folds of the portière.

"There is no heart trouble," the Englishman assured him with a smile. "It is a
question of naturalization. Doctor Tsarka
will not object to an examination of his
papers."

Pepio spoke three words in the vernacular
to the shadow in the portière, then, with a
kindling eye, faced Renwick.

"We people of Japan are led to believe
that an Englishman's house is his castle.
It seems," she added tartly, "that the home
of a Japanese gentleman may be invaded
at any time by a lot of stupid officials!"

The shadow in the portière beckoned
Gifford. "Doctor Tsarka will your questions
answer. That girl," he wagged a nicotine-
blackened finger at Pepio, "has the devil's
temper got. She is the seventh daughter of
a learned man. Unlucky as opals these
sevenths," he supplemented vaguely. "Come
along."

Gifford followed with a dim sense of having
created rather an inextricable situation, while
Pepio stormed at the doorkeeper for permitting
the white man to force his way upon them at
so late an hour.

"Come along!" The Jap swung from the

passage into another room, where Renwick's astonished eyes fell upon a collection of disused Bunsen cells piled against the wall. A square table filled the centre of the apartment, and on it were littered a number of glass bulbs and tubes containing Magdala red, "thaleen" and hydro-carbon. The walls were covered with Japanese articles of curious workmanship and design. The floor was without carpet or linoleum, and revealed numerous acid stains on its bare surface.

Gifford marvelled now, as he followed the little Jap, that the Scotland Yard officials had allowed Doctor Tsarka's premises to go unsearched. His conductor led him down a flight of stone steps into a garden that faced Professor Moritz's laboratory from the western side.

The air smelt dank and conveyed an impression of vitriol residues and carelessly handled chemical washes. A high wall surrounded the garden, damp and moss-grown where the overhanging trees shut out the windows of the adjoining houses.

"My master everywhere sleeps but in the house," his attendant informed him. "He is troubled with the street noises — the dogs, the newsboys that make disturbance with their face."

"And your master is a prominent nerve specialist!" Gifford laughed as the Jap halted before the shut door of a newly painted outbuilding.

"The physic man is always not a good healer of himself," grunted the attendant. "There are noises in my poor head that he cannot put in tune. In go now and speak of the things that are of great annoyance to you."

Thrusting open the main door of the outbuilding, Gifford entered with his conductor, and his alert senses became conscious of a heavily ionized atmosphere impregnated with the fumes of strong tobacco.

The Jap vanished from his side, leaving him staring into the blackness of the flat-roofed outbuilding. In all his life Gifford had never known fear. He had encountered riverside desperadoes and fleet-footed bank smashers by the score, yet there had never come to him the feeling of unknown terror, which passed like the beating of a vulture's wing.

Slowly, imperceptibly he became aware of a

face reviewing him almost at arm's length, and then of a huge squat shape that seemed to leap from the ground gripping him wrist and throat.

Gifford's right fist smashed past the elusive face, and again with trip-hammer force as he sought to beat away the encircling arms of his unseen adversary.

Across the floor he reeled, panting like a lion in the grip of a python. No sound came from either, until a soft spongy mass was pressed over his eyes and quickly withdrawn. A savage grunt of satisfaction ensued; then a door closed on his right, leaving the young detective panting and mystified, unable to comprehend the nature of the mysterious assault.

A sudden strain of laughter echoed through the darkness, followed by the unmistakable click of an electric button. Instantly the apartment was inundated with a powerful light that revealed to his astonished eyes an oblong room furnished and upholstered to suit the fancy of a Piccadilly exquisite or art connoisseur.

At the extreme end of the room, beneath a cloudwork of tapestry and screens, stood a scarlet embroidered ottoman with a heavy brass reading lamp at the head. Under the lamp, tucked among the piled-up cushions, lay a small, wizened figure in a yellow dressing gown. For an instant there flashed upon Renwick all the weird stories of dwarfs and elves he had ever read. The figure on the ottoman differed from the picture-book goblins only in the cast of its features — it was Japanese, and very much amused at the manner of his entry.

"I beg your pardon," Gifford began, bracing himself like one recovering from a severe shock; "the attendant informed me that I should meet Doctor Tsarka."

The figure on the ottoman leaned forward, revealing a pair of narrow shoulders and tight-fitting skull-cap.

"I am Doctor Tsarka. My *confrère*, Horubu, treated you rather roughly, I fancy," he said in decisive tones. "Horubu is troubled with apparations. He mistook you probably for an anarchist."

There was malice in the last word, and in the brief pause that followed Gifford studied the capacious brow and rather well-formed features under the creaseless skull-cap. He

felt instinctively that he was under the surveillance of a master criminal, a man frail
of body, but whose very presence exuded the
Titanic energies of his mind.   Yet the Englishman, impressed   as   he   was   by   Doctor
Tsarka's personality,   could   scarcely   repress
a smile at his diminutive figure and mock
serious pose.

The   little   doctor   interrupted   his   swift
thoughts by rising from the ottoman and
assuming a Napoleonic attitude beside the
brass reading lamp.

"Your business here is one that might very
well have   been   discussed   with   my   Consul
in London.   You   have   commited   a   grevious
blunder, my young friend, a blunder that may
cost you many sleepless nights."

Renwick was   aware   of   a   slight   stinging
sensation across both eyes, accompanied by
flashes of purple light across the retina.   Each
attempt to open his eyes was rewarded with
a series of needle-like pricks that caused him
almost to cry out.

A sigh of regret escaped the little nerve
specialist as he regarded the flinching figure
before him.

"You   will   grow   accustomed   to   the   illuminations after a while," he affirmed. "There will be green rays and violet mists; you will also suffer from irruptions of ultramarine. Personally, I can recommend the green rays," he added facetiously. "They suit the complexion of most young Englishmen."

Gifford with a sick taste in his mouth, groped his way to a chair, his left hand upraised to shield his eyes from the penetrating glare of the electric bulb overhead.

"The illuminations are certainly startling!" He spoke huskily, his hand gripping the chairback to steady his shaking limbs. "May I ask if that sponge affair, that was squeezed over my eyes, contained anything poisonous?"

"My *confrère*, Horubu, is capable of anything when his liberty is threatened," was the unimpassioned rejoinder. "He anticipated your coming."

Gifford rocked forward, pressed his fingers tightly over his closed eyes as though to stay the flame of torment that seared his optic nerves. It occurred to him that he had fallen among a gang of medical fiends. His other speculations concerning the whereabouts of Moritz's lost radium were obliterated by the curious phenomena of light-rays through which he was passing.

Doctor Tsarka addressed him sullenly. "You came here to arrest me or my daughter, to drag us to one of your beastly gaols. For days past you have followed Pepio San, bribing her chauffeur to slow down whenever you gave a signal from your own car!"

Gifford was considering the slender veins of ultramarine and scarlet that shot across his throbbing brain. Each effort to meet Doctor Tsarka's glance brought fresh stabs of pain, until the apartment seemed to dissolve in a volcano of blinding flame.

There were possibilities in the situation which caused him to ponder helplessly. The thought of blindness left him cold. Men in his profession had been rendered inert by the use of anæsthetics. It had been left to the Oriental mind to invent a new alternative in the way of balking unwelcome investigations.

The little Japanese doctor breathed near his face, betraying a certain professional curiosity.

"The eye of a man is a wonderful instrument," he volunteered. "It deludes the brain and fills the heart with immeasurable joy or torment."

Gifford winced. It seemed as though an eagle's claw had fastened upon his eyes. To move backward or forward became an undertaking of considerable peril. The room had become absorbed in the volcano of purple rays. Only the electric bulb above his head was visible; the figure of Doctor Tsarka was a mere gnome-like blur, a goblin shadow that gesticulated — and smoked a cigarette.

"You were unfortunate enough to walk into my operating theatre when my *confrère*, Horubu, was conducting an experiment in molecular activity," the little nerve doctor explained. "Your eyes have been filamented. One of these days the light may return to you. Until then your future is at my disposal."

By stretching out his hand Gifford might have squeezed the breath from the imp-like figure beside him. He restrained his desire with an effort, knowing that any attempt at violence would bring a horde of Japanese house-servants about his ears.

The pat, pat, of Tsarka's sandalled feet sounded across the apartment. Then fol-

lowed the unmistakable sound of a type-
writer, and Renwick knew that the little
nerve specialist was manipulating the key-
board of an up-to-date machine. It ceased,
and he heard the flutter of notepaper at
his elbow.

"You will sign this letter, my friend,"
the little doctor spoke close to his ear. "It
is addressed to your employer."

Gifford shrugged. "Read it out," he said
huskily.

Doctor Tsarka paused to make a slight
correction with his pencil; then in a clear
voice read the message:

"DEAR SIR — I have stumbled unexpectedly upon a piece
of information which may assist in clearing up the Moritz
case. The 'clue' is on his way to Paris this evening. I
follow. Will wire results in a day or two.
'Yours, etc."

Doctor Tsarka placed the letter in his hand.
"Oblige by appending your signature. It may
save you from another bombardment of violet
rays. Savvy?"

Gifford's fingers closed on the note. Tsarka's
first move now was to prevent other detectives following on his heels. He put down
the paper.

"I do not feel inclined to sign my own death

warrant, Doctor Tsarka. Suppose we allow
things to take their course?"

"The course would be distinctly unpleasant
for you. Now," the little doctor wheeled
upon him suddenly, "you have a friend named
Hackett. Does he know that you come here?"

"He may have guessed. We often guess
each other's intentions without asking."

"Good; then you must sign. I promise no
further harm to you. Yet . . .   By the
gods if you do not!" Renwick felt the frail
body pulsate beside him as the small, wiry
fingers clutched his sleeve.

"Fire away!" Gifford exclaimed passionately. "You have struck your worst blow.
Let the game go on!"

The Japanese doctor retreated, then paused
at a distance to contemplate the erect, white
figure in the centre of the apartment. The
folding-screen at his elbow moved aside; a
face pressed into the light and stared with
Tsarka at the immobile young detective.

"Go away . . .   thou!" The doctor
snapped his fingers at the face. "This affair is
mine, Satalaya!"

The face vanished. Doctor Tsarka inclined
his head. "Do not drive me to extremes,"

he continued, addressing Renwick. "I bear
you no malice. Put your hand to this paper.
The pen is here."

"Do you intend to keep me in this place?"

"You shall be my guest for two days,
not an hour longer. If you attempt to leave
without permission —— "

"Well?"

Doctor Tsarka made a litte noise in his
throat that was neither a laugh nor a cry.

"Why do you wish to die unpleasantly?"
he asked after a pause. "It is not heroic.
If I struck you with half a million volts no
one would hear a noise. Be sane; there is
no audience here to applaud your determination. Take this paper and sign!"

Renwick remained standing in the centre
of the apartment like one counting his own
heartbeats.

"I want to ask you, Doctor Tsarka, whether
this," he touched his eyes suggestively, "is
a mere illusion or a total eclipse of the vision?
Does it mean blindness for me?"

"It is not an illusion," was the swift response. "You will henceforth walk in
darkness unless certain remedies are applied
within a few days."

Gifford nodded, and then, clearing his voice, spoke again.

"What do you mean by certain remedies?" he questioned. "An ordinary oculist could repair the damage — don't you think?"

Doctor Tsarka salaamed facetiously to the half-blind figure before him. "There is only one person in England capable of rendering you service. She is a student of the new science of radio-magnetics."

Again Renwick nodded. "So, unless I sign this letter, you intend keeping me here until I am past hope?"

"Sign it!" came sharply from the Japanese doctor. "We people of Nippon love brave men; the stupid ones we adorn with asses' ears!"

"Give me the paper, and guide my hand, O man of little iniquities!"

He thrust out his fingers with a blind gesture.

Doctor Tsarka guided his hand over the paper, and after scrutinizing the signature, carefully placed the letter in an envelope. With scarcely a sound he moved toward the maze of screens and slipped from the apartment.

CHAPTER II

A GREAT silence came over the apartment, and Gifford waited, like a trapped lion, for something to move toward him. In his experience of London's Asiatic criminal population, he had encountered nothing which destroyed his self-control so completely as the momentary pressure of Horubu's radium-sponge, for he was convinced now that the Jap had manipulated some radio-active substance during their short wrestling bout.

The question of his mission to the house of the Japanese nerve specialist vanished at the thought of his peculiar predicament. Of the misfortunes which afflicted mankind he dreaded blindness most. He barely restrained himself from crying out as he listened for a sound to penetrate the stillness of Doctor Tsarka's operating theatre.

During those waiting moments Gifford's despair was very real. At the outset of his career he had been practically struck down by a hand skilled in the deadly uses of radio-surgery. His blindness might be transitory, or it might walk with him through life. And he had looked forward to a career which promised enduring rewards, for to him the suppression of criminality had become a religion into which he had plunged, giving heart and brain to the service.

His father, a retired army captain, had died, leaving an encumbered estate and a wife whose early training unfitted her for the strife of existence. So Gifford had taken up the burden, in his twenty-second year, determined to win for the gray-haired mother competency and respite from life's daily struggle. Failure, white and pitiless, had leaped to meet him. The unravelling of the Moritz radium mystery, which had already blighted the careers of several Scotland Yard experts, had caught him in its toils.

Gifford's desire to recover the lost radium tube had been kindled by the fact that Professor Moritz was labouring to abolish the most dreaded of human scourges. He was aware that Eugene Moritz could never replace the precious material which had contributed so vitally to his researches.

Doctor Tsarka returned unexpectedly, his slight frame palpitating with good-humoured excitement.

"Now that your letter has been posted, Mr. Renwick, we may assume a more hospitable attitude."

Reaching a cigar box from a near shelf, he proffered it with a smile.

"You will find them excellent for the nerves," he vouchsafed; "although scientists have not yet proclaimed tobacco an antidote for radium poisoning."

Gifford accepted a cigar and half stumbled into a chair, while the knife blade sensation in his temples soon gave way under the soothing influence of the weed.

Doctor Tsarka contented himself with a gold-tipped cigarette. Lying back on the ottoman he regarded Renwick smilingly.

"I am sorry that my *confrère* subjected you to the sponge. You will understand that his action arose from a desire to protect himself and me from the police."

"It was my duty to investigate and bring about an arrest if possible," Gifford admitted.

The Jap laughed easily, while the slow-lifting smoke oozed from his lips.

"You came for Moritz's radium, and you received a few filaments through the nerve passages of your eyes."

Gifford barely repressed himself. "Why . . . you admit that it is in your possession!" was all he could say.

Tsarka twirled his cigarette between his finger and thumb until it resembled a fiery wheel.

"You will spend your life in proving the fact," he purred. "Yet Horubu used it to advantage."

"In blinding me!" Gifford affirmed. "It was a noble thought, Doctor Tsarka!"

"It was certainly a dramatic one." The little Japanese specialist manipulated his fiery wheel with impish dexterity. Not for an instant did his eyes wander from the crouching figure in the chair.

"We Japanese take no chances in life," he went on. "At the first sign of the tiger's claw we strike — hard!"

Gifford sighed. "Please regard me as a paper tiger in future," he said with a touch of bitterness. "The real article would have

shot you and your sponge-waving Horubu
at sight."

An outburst of merriment greeted his words.
Tsarka, in his exuberance, kicked his sandalled feet against the ottoman, while the skin
of his face creased like hammered bronze.

"You have emotion, but no head balance,
Mr. Renwick. It is well that you did not
attempt violence."

A shadow crossed his face, a livid hatred
that was gone in a breath.

"Some of us prefer to die out of prison,"
he went on. "Horubu and myself are taking
no chances."

Gifford smoked in silence while the knife-
stabs in his temple grew less deadly. The
Japanese doctor's strange admissions puzzled
him. It was seldom that an Asiatic implicated himself voluntarily. But the young
detective knew enough of the Oriental mind,
its vain inconsistencies and deceits, to at-
tribute much importance to Tsarka's gratuitous statements.

He was not disposed, however, to stem the
tide of information which floated oil-like from
the little man's lips.

He leaned from his chair, his left hand

drawn across his eyes. "Doctor Tsarka, let me frankly pay tribute to your genius and knowledge. When a foreigner manages to baffle the combined wits of England's criminal investigators, one has to pay homage."

His shot appeared to kindle Tsarka's dormant vanity. The little man gestured with his cigarette.

"I have been amused by the attitude of Scotland Yard in regard to the Moritz case. That some of its officers are stupid goes without saying."

"You have been very clever," the Englishman admitted, "to drive to the verge of distraction the most brilliant men of our time."

"We succeeded, Mr. Renwick, because you men have no imaginations. They go to work like blacksmiths seeking to disentangle a handful of gossamer threads. Listen!"

Something warned Gifford that the Japanese doctor was in the humour for disclosures. He smoked furiously, scarce daring to interrupt the thread of the little man's discourse. With all his silence and duplicity Doctor Tsarka's pulses throbbed for the

Englishman's praise. In the security of his own house his Asian vanity leaped and cried for applause.

"You English are very clever; you are big and brave; you go to war like lions with unbroken teeth, but," he lay back on the otto-man, his eyes glinting in suppressed merri-ment, "you have no imagination. You have not learned to think as little children think. If you see a daisy in the field it is only a daisy to you — nothing more."

"What would you call it?" Renwick in-terposed.

Doctor Tsarka shrugged. "To the eye of the child it may be something more — a fairy's cap, or a drop of gold in the eye of a waking elf, but it is never a daisy. We Japanese are not grown up. To us the 12-inch gun is still a dragon of war, ready to thunder its message of death at the enemies of our people. And . . . so, when we bring our child-brain into our schemes we leave an institution like Scotland Yard agape at what they are pleased to call an unfath-omable mystery."

Gifford yawned a trifle wearily. He had expected more from the little doctor. "The mountain rumbles and the mouse comes forth," he said in his disappointment.

"No; a rat!" Tsarka chuckled audibly, and again the cigarette became a wheel of fire between his nimble thumb and forefinger. "It was a very small rat that broke the hearts of a score of London's most brilliant detectives when they sought to elucidate the Moritz mystery," he continued.

"On the day that the Professor acquired his six grains of radium the newspapers informed us of the circumstance. For more than a year I had followed closely the results of his experiments in cancer research. It was an open secret, too, that Lord St. Ellesmayne, President of the Cancer Research Society, had presented him with the radium. Well, to be frank with you, I wanted those six grains of radium to complete a little experiment of my own. I could not afford, however, to put up the sum of money required for its purchase. The fact that my house adjoins Moritz's, and that his laboratory stands within twenty feet of this apartment, set me thinking how I might borrow the whole of the precious radium without his knowledge."

Doctor Tsarka paused to light another

cigarette, and the match-glow illumined his eyes with a peculiar metallic brilliance.

"Now we come to the Japanese child intelligence when it is directed against an apparently impossible task," he continued. "A thought came to me that was suggested by the reading of one of Narcrissino's fables — the Japanese poet of the Seven Lakes. It was the story of the Dragon and the Rat. Mentally, I put Moritz in the Dragon's castle because he held the flaming witch-fires I so badly needed for my own experiments.

"Horubu, after much worry and expense, obtained a plan of Moritz's house from the architect who built it. It enabled us to study it carefully, and we found that it would be impossible to enter his laboratory without killing every member of his household and leaving traces of our presence everywhere around. So we studied his drains and brought little Kezzio into the game."

"Kezzio?" Renwick leaned forward toward the ottoman. "Who is Kezzio?" he inquired innocently.

Tsarka's eyes were pinched to narrow slits of light as he responded:

"Kezzio is the white rat from Nagasaki.
It was given to me by a worker in magic
named Sere Sani."

Renwick peered forward in astonishment.
"You, Tsarka the scientist, talk of workers
in magic!"

"Sere Sani was a harmless fellow," Tsarka
continued unmoved, "with his gilt paper
wands and the medicated flower bulbs which
grew while you waited. We took the rat
Kezzio, because it had the brains of a man-
child and the tricks of a sewer thief.

"It learned more tricks from us after we
had studied the water pipes leading from
Moritz's laboratory. Horubu discovered that
they joined ours where the house wall and
the garden meet. My pipes reach my neigh-
bour's on the right, Moritz's meet ours on
the left.

"All his residues and chemical washes ran
through our garden drain. An idea came
to me, one day, when I opened the drain to
analyze his runaway washes. Like Madame
Curie, I was anxious to know what my brother
scientist was throwing away. I picked up
several large pieces of nickel salts, and from
these I gathered that his sink pipe had no

screen. And so the thought of sending Kezzio into his laboratory, by way of the sink pipe, came to me."

Renwick half rose from his seat and then sat down abruptly. "The thing is childish, absurd!" he muttered under his breath.

"Moritz had regular working hours," Doctor Tsarka went on, with a placid smile in Renwick's direction. "From experience we gathered in many English laboratories, we felt confident that the glass tube containing his radium supply was constantly at his elbow.

"We had a large working model of his laboratory, and we knew from his shadow near the barred window that he conducted most of his experiments on a marble-faced bench that stood against the wall. Beside it was a white stone sink fitted with hot and cold water taps.

"Well, we began by sending Kezzio up the model pipe to the marble-faced bench that represented the exact spot where Moritz placed his radium tube whenever he crossed the laboratory to answer a call at the telephone.

"At first Kezzio did not like the wet journey up the pipe. A little starving and coaxing made him alter his mind. In less than a week he began to understand something of his task."

"Task!" Renwick allowed the hot cigar ash to fall on his knee. "Surely you do not mean —— " He paused as though a blade of light had entered his throbbing eyes, both hands pressed over his brow. "Go on," he ventured in a steady voice. "I beg your pardon, Doctor Tsarka."

The little specialist nodded amiably.

"We taught the rat to pick up a glass tube that held a few sparks of phosphorus, and return with it down a curved pipe. To you the trick may seem foolish and incredible, having a thousand chances of failure against it. But we Japanese are a patient people, and there is not a trick on earth that a well-trained rat is not capable of attempting. Rodents have carried off diamond rings and bracelets from the dressing tables of the rich. History is strewn with stories of jewel thefts perpetrated by mischievous house rats whose love of bright objects is keener than most women's."

Doctor Tsarka paused to hug his knees as the thought of his daring experiment thrilled his blood.

"Few men ever played with the brain of a rat as we played. How many have studied the ordinary rat's capacity for trick work as we Japanese? The brain of a healthy rodent is as impressionable as wax or gold; it is quicker than a dog to understand, and, above all other living animals, it possesses an innate love of bright metal and glittering objects. Kezzio, after a few days' practice, would pick up a glass tube of phosphorus and carry it down a wet pipe at a signal from me or my companion, Horubu.

"Only by Moritz's shadow crossing the window could we see when he was at work. We were just a bit afraid of his chemical washes coming down the pipe, for we did not care to send little Kezzio to his death. To be caught in the drain when Moritz was throwing out cyanide water or a solution of sulphuric acid would have been a very unpleasant experience for the rat.

"Moritz's telephone cleared the way. If we could keep him talking a while with his face from the marble-topped bench, Kezzio would have a chance of proving his worth.

"On August 18th, about eleven o'clock in the morning, Horubu rang up Professor Moritz from the British Medical Insitute and held him in conversation for several minutes. Horubu had been reading up Pultowa's book on radio-magnetics, and he was able to interest the professor on the light energy of disintegrated molecules.

"I became aware of Moritz's presence at the telephone through the medium of an electric appliance which notified me from one of my own wires.

"I was sitting in the garden, near the severed drain pipe, with Kezzio held in my right hand. There had been a slight flush of water a few moments before, but I trusted that no more would come down while Moritz was at the receiver.

"The rat seemed to understand my intense anxiety as I knelt by the open pipe. Its ears went back and its eyes turned to me bright and questioning. 'Up, little man,' I said, and thrust him into the pipe.

"You may think it was a silly experiment, the result of an opium dream, or childish fancy; but we Japanese are only children, and we sometimes accomplish the incredible by our passionate interest in everything we undertake

"Kezzio was gone not more than thirty-five seconds when his wet nose came pointing from the pipe end. Something was wrong, and the priceless moments were flying. Horubu could not keep Moritz at the telephone a minute longer. I looked quickly at Kezzio and saw that its paws were burnt with acid residues. Dipping them in oil (it was ready at my elbow), I wiped the tiny claws swiftly and with a tweak of the ears sent it into the pipe.

"I was hopeful that Moritz would not return from the telephone, for I knew that his approach would scare Kezzio from the laboratory. I received a signal from one of my assistants, posted at the upstairs window, telling me that the professor had hung up the receiver and was about to return to his work.

"Kezzio's burnt feet had spoilt our calculations I felt certain. Kneeling on the ground I peered into the severed pipe and waited. The pipe was quite black inside and smelt strongly of nitrate solutions and bitter chemical residues. As I looked within I saw a strange thing. From the darkness there came a burning star of light that glowed in the damp drain with the power of a live sunbeam. Never before had I seen so curious a spectacle as this starry flame that came foot by foot toward me. It was Kezzio, and the little fellow tumbled into my hand with six thousand pounds' worth of radium. The glass tube that held it was hardly bigger than your finger."

Renwick's head had fallen forward during the latter half of the Japanese doctor's story. His half-smoked cigar smouldered on the ash tray beside him. Tsarka eyed him sympathetically, then rose suddenly from the ottoman and touched the bent shoulders.

"You had better rest a while. After all my narrative has only bored you. There is a comfortable room adjoining this one. My servant will show you the way. Sleep a little. To-morrow you may feel better."

Pressing an electric button in the wall he returned with a sigh to his couch.

Renwick strove to clear his brain from the clouding effects of the cigar. "Your rat story would read well in a child's picture book, Doctor Tsarka," he said with an effort. "One could scarcely expect a man of the world to believe it."

"Will your employer believe your story

of Horubu's radium sponge when you return
to him?" Tsarka faced him with the agility
of a dancing master. "Or will he interpret
it as an effort on your part to achieve a little
newspaper notoriety?"

The young detective winced. "A man does
not blind himself to earn a few press notices,"
he retorted.   "The world would certainly
smile if I submitted your rat and water-pipe
espisode for judgment."

"You—you consider it a little too Jappy?"
the doctor queried. "Well, so be it. Scotland Yard has yet to put forward a saner
theory concerning the theft of Moritz's radium.
Try a good sleep.   I will not bore you with
my silly stories in future."

A coolie servant entered, and at a nod
from his master conducted Renwick into the
adjoining room. The windows opened upon
the high-walled garden below, and Gifford
felt the night air blowing in from an overhead
fanlight as he moved forward gingerly. Without a word the coolie locked the door from the
outside, leaving him standing in the centre of
the apartment.

Groping right and left he discovered a
small table and chair near the window.   In

a far corner was a small camp bed that smelt of stale cigars and strange clothing. A carafe of water stood on the table; he drank greedily and spilled a little on the cloth before he was aware of the fact.

The water revived him and set him thinking of his helpless plight. Setting out only a few hours before with the determination to solve the Moritz radium' mystery he had fallen an easy victim to Japanese art and trickery. His credulity had been tested to the utmost by the little doctor's astounding confession of the theft, together with his weirdly fascinating account of the rat's entry into Professor Moritz's laboratory.

The coolie servant returned with some food which Renwick put aside, contenting himself with a single cup of coffee. He slept a little, and woke with the booming of a church clock in his ears. He was also conscious of a presence in the room of a soft-footed shape breathing near the doorway.

"Who are you?" he called out. "What do you want?"

"I came to look at you. I could not sleep because I feel that something has happened. Are — are you hurt?"

It was Pepio's voice. He sat up on the camp bed striving to pierce the velvet darkness that surrounded him.

"Your people dealt very promptly with me," he confessed grimly. "They took everything except my life."

"Horubu would have killed you only for my father," she whispered. "What . . . miserable destiny brought you here?"

He caught a faint sobbing in her voice that struck like steel upon his nerves. "Destiny had nothing to do with it," he answered bluntly. "It was my business."

He felt her moving nearer, nearer, until her laboured breathing sounded almost in his ear. Some strange emotion was upon her, he felt certain, the curiosity of the gaoleress to gaze upon the prisoner. An aroma of violets and mignonette swam with her; the tinkle, tinkle, of her gold wrist ornaments was an epic in the silence.

She paused near him, breathing quickly. "Something is wrong with your eyes," she whispered. "You — you are not looking at me!"

Her voice held a peculiar childish sweetness and innocence, but the note of terror in it

leaped at him with the precision of a death
warrant.

He put up his hand awkwardly as though
he would brush away the envelope of darkness
that cut him off from the world.

"A touch of radium blindness," he vouchsafed. "You know it was that fellow Horubu,
as you call him, put a sponge over my eyes."
He lowered his hand mechanically. "Did
you turn on the light?" he asked.

Her answer was not very clear to him. As
far as he could judge she was standing somewhere in the centre of the room, and the
moments seemed to pulsate between her childlike sobbing.

"I am so sorry; oh, so sorry!" The silence
fell again leaving him wondering whether the
daughter of Terino Tsarka was really in league
with the gang of Asiatic ruffians who appeared
to swarm about the house.

"When I have an enemy," he spoke through
his shut teeth now, "I shall pray for him to
descend into this inferno of colour where red
rays cannonade the nerves like grape shot."

His face turned upward suddenly. "Pepio
Tsarka," he asked hoarsely; "is there a
light in this room?"

"Yes." Her answer came with a sob. It was inconceivable that this Japanese girl should feel sorry for him. An hour before he was ready to arrest her on a charge of theft. It was humiliating to be wept over by the daughter of a professional burglar (he could not regard Doctor Tsarka in any other light). His breath came quickly as he turned to her again.

"Tell me, Pepio San, do you know anything of a — a rodent called Kezzio?"

The sobbing ceased instantly; he heard again the quick movement of her gold wrist ornaments as though her hands had come together suddenly.

"A white rat," he urged with a suppressed grimace, "that enters people's houses by way of the sink pipes?"

"My father keeps one," she admitted frankly, "and its name is Kezzio. I never heard of it entering any one's house though," she added innocently.

"Thank you, Pepio San. It was very foolish of me to come here. Now," he paused again, his lips parted good humouredly, "can you tell me, Pepio, whether my life is safe here?"

"Are you an Englishman, afraid of death?" was her unexpected query.

Renwick's unsuppressed mirth betrayed his boyish nature. "When I am as old as your father, Pepio, I shall probably welcome it. But at twenty-three I am interested in life. I have work to do. Also, if I may mention it, Pepio San, I am vastly attached to a little white-haired Englishwoman about sixty years of age."

"Your mother?"

"Yes, Pepio, my mother. She is a very particular little person, and would resent any one taking my life."

"Some one else cares besides your mother?"

"I think not, Pepio. In England we cleave to our parents, as you cleave to yours."

"Then you are not rich enough to marry?" was her next question. "And so you cling to your mother."

"Exactly; but there won't be any more clinging, Pepio, if I'm carefully garotted or bow-strung during the night. What do you think?"

She retreated to the door without responding. A voice was calling her in the passage, a deep-throated voice that sounded like some terrible echo from a forest.

Renwick strove to make out the strange volley of oaths that followed the young Japanese girl as she hurried away. The heavy footsteps halted at his door, he heard the key turned savagely in the lock, accompanied by a string of ferocious remarks uttered in Japanese. The heavy feet tramped away and as he listened he caught the sound of Doctor Tsarka's voice remonstrating with his daughter for daring to visit the man whose presence in the house had threatened their liberty.

CHAPTER III

DURING the night Renwick was kept awake by the sound of men's feet in the passage, accompanied by dragging noises suggestive of heavy furniture being removed to a van in the street. Toward daybreak he fell into a sleep that was disturbed by the occasional slamming of a door or the dropping of some metal utensil on the stone floor outside.

He awoke with a bitter taste in his mouth, a splitting pain over the eyes as though a sharp-bladed instrument had penetrated to the nerves. A glass of water from the carafe steadied him slightly. Groping his way to a chair he listened for some indication of life about the house, his mind obsessed by the curious experience of the last few hours.

Something of the city's stir pierced the heavy walls of his apartment, the unmistakable roar of motor traffic, the far-off whistle of a passing locomotive. Sound did not easily traverse the long corridors leading to Doctor Tsarka's sleeping quarters. The rear part of the house descended twenty feet below the level of the street. The garden itself was a mere grassy, well-like enclosure. All thought of breaking from the house had been abandoned by Renwick the moment his sight had failed.

Given a possible chance he would have fought his way into the road, at the outset. No chance had offered. The trained dependants of the little Japanese doctor had not thought fit to relieve him of his revolver. In the house of an enemy a blind man becomes less menacing than a beetle or garden tortoise.

Renwick could only fret and grope his way from window to table, pausing at times to listen for a footstep in the passage outside.

He had hoped that Pepio San might return. Even her voice was better than the terrible silence. He was just beginning to realize the effects of the radium sponge. Complete darkness assailed him. The faint nimbus of light which had penetrated the black void had vanished utterly. He had only the Japanese doctor's assurance that a genuine specific for radium blindness existed. But deep in

Renwick's consciousness was the fixed idea that the sponge-wielder had dealt with him finally. There would be no resurrection from the awful pit of gloom into which he had been cast. The Japanese gang of thieves had made sure that he would never appear against them. It would be left to Tony Hackett to follow where his investigations had ceased.

The sound of a broom in the passage sent him to the door listening eagerly. Nearer came the sound until it stopped at Doctor Tsarka's room. A pail was banged heavily on the floor. Then a key was thrust into the lock of his door and opened briskly.

Renwick stepped back, his guard arm raised slightly. "Who are you?" he asked hoarsely. "Are you Pepio San?"

The intruder breathed warily as though the shock of meeting was quite unexpected. It was a woman's voice that spoke, a brogue-mellowed voice that eased the strain on his mind.

"Shure I came to clane up the empty house, sorr. I'd no idea there was a gentleman insoide."

There was no doubt in his mind concerning the personality of the visitor. He had

met the London housecleaner and charwoman
before. He took a step to the open door,
scarce believing his senses.

"I want to go from here," he said quickly.
"The late occupants have taken everything
from the house I suppose?"

"There's not a stick left but what stands
in this room, sorr. 'Tis yourself that looks
sick an' troubled, if I may take the liberty
of sayin' it."

Renwick felt called upon to explain his
presence in the empty house. A sudden
step forward brought him with a bump
against the passage wall. He turned, swear-
ing a little under his breath, in the direction
of the charwoman's voice.

"I met with an accident here last night.
Perhaps",—he searched his pockets and drew
out a half-crown — "perhaps you would be
good enough to lead me to the street. My
eyesight is not very good to-day."

A faint gasp of surprise greeted his admission. The charwoman's broom fell to the
floor instantly. Her hand sought his sleeve
and drew him along the passage into the
garden toward the house. They passed up
the steps through the glass-roofed conserva-

tory where he had noted the rows of chemical jars and glass bulbs. The air of the street blew upon him the moment she opened the front door. He halted on the steps uncertainly like one afraid to plunge unescorted into the maelstrom of London traffic.

He turned to the breathing figure beside him, a final question on his lips. "Did you see Doctor Tsarka go from here?" he asked.

"No, sorr; 'twas the house agent, Mr. Jenner, that sent me here."

"But the house was only vacant this morning." He fingered his watch chain undecidedly. "Mr. Jenner did not lose much time in sending you to clean up," he added with a touch of suspicion.

"I was cleaning the front of the house all yesterday," came unexpectedly from the Irishwoman. "'Twould have been small trouble to let you out, sorr, if I had known."

Gifford held himself a trifle desperately. "To-day is only Thursday!" he broke out. "I came in here last evening, Wednesday, just before midnight!"

The charwoman laughed in spite of herself. "Askin' your pardon, sorr, the day is Friday. 'Twas an egg I had for breakfast instead av me usual rasher av bacon."

Gifford gestured impatiently. "Call a cab; there should be one at the street corner."

Stumbling down the steps he waited, chafing at each moment's delay, until the charwoman succeeded in hailing a taxi. With the driver's assistance he gained a seat, and was soon on his way to his employer's office.

He could not conceal his disgust at the inexplicable passage of time. His exhausted nerves had no doubt succumbed to the shock of the radium sponge, or it may have been that some unknown drug in his coffee had contributed to his long sleep.

Arriving at the office, the chauffeur assisted him to alight. The voice of Tony Hackett was heard singing on the stairs as Renwick stumbled into view. No one had ever met Tony on the stairs without hearing the latest music-hall ditty warbled in a soft, tenor voice. The song ceased in mid-octave as Renwick halted, groping on the stairhead, and changed to a whistle of surprise.

"Drunk, by Jove!" Tony's hand closed on Renwick's shoulder and drew him unceremoniously into a side room. "Where have you been? Man alive, you are not going into the chief's room in that state!"

Renwick's appearance warranted Tony's suspicions. The unshaven face, the tight, pain-drawn mouth and, above all, the half-closed eyes that bore a curious silver scar across the lids.

Hackett caught his breath sharply.

"What is it, Renny . . . Something whipped you over the eyes?"

Renwick steadied himself with an effort.

"I blundered into a crowd of Japanese nerve-tappers. They fixed me up for two nights and got away. I want to see the chief. Pass me in, Tony."

Anthony Coleman, the head of the famous detective agency, received the young man with the customary nod.

"We understood that you had gone to Paris," he said briefly. "You seem to have been in trouble." He made a gesture to the stooping figure before him. "Sit down."

Renwick groped to a chair, his radium-seared eyes turned toward the grizzled man with the authoritative voice. Briefly enough he outlined the cause of his absence, embracing, in a few short sentences, the story of his experiences in the house of the Japanese nerve specialist.

Anthony Coleman listened pensively without exhibiting the slightest trace of surprise or emotion. His steely eyes flashed once or twice during the short narrative, while his fingers wandered from time to time toward a pigeon-hole in his desk where the name Tsarka had been indexed with a number of others.

"Your impulsiveness has not increased our chances of getting this nerve quack," he vouchsafed at the conclusion of Renwick's story. "The radium thieves are probably now on their way to America. So much for personal initiative," he snapped.

Thrusting a handful of papers into a near drawer, he permitted himself a close survey of the young man who had failed after so much brilliant theoretical work to bring the Moritz case to a close.

"Are you quite blind?" he asked. "Can't you see anything?"

Renwick shrugged a trifle wearily. "I fancy my working days are over, sir. I am sorry you are disappointed with my work. Things do not always come into line when we expect them; leastways, the Japanese won't," he added grimly.

Anthony Coleman shifted uneasily in his chair. "I think you had better consult an oculist," he said, with a side glance toward the door. "I'll ring up Sir Floyd Garston. He does a lot of work for the Scotland Yard men. Get a cab and," he glanced again at the stooping, gray-faced young man in the chair, "and pull yourself together, Renwick," he added, with a shade of pity in his voice.

Outside, Gifford was taken charge of by the irrepressible Tony Hackett. As they descended the steps together the cherubic little detective drew a letter from his pocket and placed it in his companion's hand.

"I got it from the office rack," he explained, "and thought of posting it to your mother. Funny writing, isn't it?" he commented innocently.

Gifford fingered the envelope, a curious smile breaking over his parched lips.

"Read it, Tony; I haven't the faintest notion who it's from."

Tony eyed the scrawled missive and read it with frequent pauses.

"DEAR FRIEND: "I promised you a physician who would repair the damage inflicted upon you by my attendant, Horubu. You will find her at No. 11 Huntingdon Street, St. James'. By going elsewhere you waste the precious moments upon which your absolute recovery depends. The name of the physician is Madame Messonier. She is skilled in radio magnetics, and is the only person in England capable of repairing the injury inflicted by my impulsive *confrère*.

"TERONI TSARKA

Hackett placed the letter in Gifford's pocket carefully. "That man has the impudence of a rhinoceros," he declared. "If ever I get on his trail I'll steady his nerves with a dose of salt and gunpowder — the little beast!"

On their way to Sir Floyd Garston's, Renwick detailed his experiences with the Japanese nerve specialist, while Hackett listened, his face to the window of the fast-moving car. He waited until his companion had finished his description of Doctor Tsarka, together with the account of the rat episode. Then Tony screwed up his lips and controlled the desire to laugh in the face of his friend.

"Those Japs have been guying you, Renny!" he declared. "But this Doctor Tsarka is rather a difficult kind of a blackguard to deal with.   There are not many of his kind within the metropolitan area, I hope."

Renwick was silent as the car threaded its way through Whitehall into Trafalgar Square.   The driver pulled up at the address given by Hackett and, without further ceremony, the two men entered the house of the famous oculist.

Anthony Coleman had evidently notified Sir Floyd Garston, for, after the briefest interval, the eminent oculist joined them in his consulting room.   A thin, hawk-faced man with an abnormal chin and brow, he appeared interested in Gifford's recital of his encounter with the radium thieves.

The silver scars on the young detective's eyelids were subjected to a searching examination.   Gifford could only feel the great man's presence as he sat still in the revolving chair, the pliant fingers that tilted his sightless face into strange light-catching angles while certain mirror-lined instruments focussed the retina of his eyes.

A great silence leaped between physician and patient, a silence that was charged with life and death for Gifford Renwick.   His mother had not yet been notified of his adventure. She still believed that he was pursuing his vocation in the City. His absence from home would in no way disconcert her, since his business often took him across Europe at the most unexpected periods.

It was the picture of this gray-haired mother that filled the black chaos of his mind. He wondered, in the waiting silence, whether they would lead him to her a stricken and hopeless derelict, or whether he would return to her roof erect and with hope in his heart.

Sir Floyd Garston remained somewhere at arm's length, a tiny steel-clad mirror in his right hand. His voice was soft, yet in the first syllable that escaped him Renwick experienced a sick, frosty feeling.

"What you have told me is truly remarkable," he began suavely. "There are indications of some radio-active agency on your retina; indeed," he breathed guardedly, as though weighing carefully the effect of his statement, "one is compelled to admit that some poisonous radio-active substance has entered the eye itself. The lids do not appear to have afforded the slightest protection."

"It — it burnt like the devil!" Renwick

spoke through his shut teeth. "Do you know much about this radio-active element?" he hazarded bluntly.

The physician's words came more distinctly, Gifford thought, and it set him wondering whether his question had outraged the great specialist's dignity.

"I — I mean that it is such unknowable stuff," he added. "No one has yet declared anything about its generative qualities."

He felt Sir Floyd's hand on his brow, and then the cool, pliant fingers on his abnormal pulse.

"One must not press too closely," the physician murmured. "I am not concerned with any radio-active theories. A general diagnosis of its effects are sufficient in the present instance."

"You think ——?"

"Ah, we must have patience. Nature is a wonderful restorer if one has command of one's self."

"About a year you think?" Renwick felt the powers of darkness closing around him; tasted of those brief moments the savage despair of the living death to be.

"One does not care to predict," Sir Floyd

responded. "Still, I shall be glad to recommend you to an ophthalmic hospital. Your case, I fear, will need patience and courage. The soldier must not quail under the knife," he added, pushing aside his instruments.

"One must attain a little of the philosophy which raises men above the assaults of pain and death."

Gifford groped for his hat in the hall, and out of the darkness around him he heard his mother's voice calling. He half turned to mutter a few words of thanks to Sir Floyd, then, with a sick, lonely feeling, surrendered himself to Tony Hackett.

"Why you're not well!" The little detective held him in the hall with more than brotherly tenderness. "Heard something nasty, eh, Renny? Come outside; the air of the street is better than the perfumes of these execution chambers."

Renwick was not given to violent attacks of self-pity, but down to the roots of his manhood he felt an unspeakable horror of the shade.

Patience and courage! Sir Floyd's words were the stock phrases of every baffled surgeon and specialist. What courage could keep him from the gulfs of despair; what patience smooth a life of blindness and premature decay?

Tony spoke words of consolation as they gained the waiting car. "Don't worry about Garston's verdict, my boy. He's pretty old when you look at him closely. Let's take a trip to the infirmary; the doctors there will fix you up."

Renwick put up a protesting hand. "Not to an infirmary, Tony. I couldn't stand that!"

"Why?" Hackett's hand fell from his shoulder; he stared blankly at the scared face of his friend. "It's the best place for you now, Renny. They'll do their utmost. There's nothing between the infirmary and going home to mother," he added with a shrug. "You won't go home until the London hospitals have turned you down."

Gifford raised his head with the jerk of a lashed steer. "We have Madame Messonier," he said huskily. "One can never tell."

"A d —— d quack!" Tony exclaimed. "I'll bet she hasn't a diploma to fly with!"

"I won't go to the infirmary!" Gifford insisted. "It is full of blind people. There

are ghosts of the dead inside its walls. I
should meet and touch other blighted souls
like myslf. I won't go there, Tony!"

Hackett swore under his breath, and spoke
to the chauffeur. "The Messonier Institute,
No. 11 Huntingdon Street. We'll see what
the lady is like, anyhow."

CHAPTER IV

THE Messonier Institute stood out in white relief against the gray-faced hospital adjoining. Within its spacious consulting rooms were suites of seagreen velvet and amethyst drapings. A liveried servant carried Gifford's card through a labyrinth of mirror-panelled apartments and returned with the intelligence that Madame's hours of consultation were limited to the early morning only. She would not, therefore, see any one.

"Be good enough to inform madame that I came at the request of Doctor Tsarka."

The attendant again departed with his message, leaving him in a state of nervous expectation.

"This Messonier woman is worth watching," whispered Tony Hackett to Gifford. "If she is in touch with Tsarka we might nab him."

Gifford sighed wearily. Only one thought lived in him now — to break through the mountainous walls of darkness and gain the light of day, to become a living entity and not a human mole.

The attendant returned full of apologies, but still austere. Madame was at that moment conducting an experiment in radio-magnetics. She could not possibly see them for another hour.

"Sounds callous and stiff-necked," Hackett growled. "If we were a couple of dukes," he added facetiously, "her ladyship would come to us in a purple flying machine, I'll wager. Deuce take the woman doctors!"

Renwick was considering his chances of recovery. And in the silence that followed Hackett became absorbed in the marvellous upholstering of the white-columned consulting room. A glance at the spacious entrance revealed an infinitude of beautifully carved stonework. Above the white enamelled doors, amid a perfect cloudwork of sculpture, leaned a robed Christ with hands spread over the blind figure of a naked man.

Hackett was struck by the mixture of Hindu and Christian symbols which permeated the modellings and frescoes. Above the wide stairs, leading to madame's private apartments, were plasters and replicas of

the Hindu gods Ganeesh and Siva. A green
bronze statue of Buddha stood in savage
silhouette against the Christ-figure on the
landing.

Only a trained observer could have picked
out the remarkable negations in the archi-
tectural feeling and design. And Tony Hackett, who possessed more than the average
detective's power of imagination, marvelled
at the weird groupings of Hindu and Christian deities. It seemed to him as though an
Oriental mind had planned the building of
the Messonier Institute.

Madame was free at last. Tony, his arm
linked in his companion's, followed the attendant into a less spacious operating room.
Hackett had expected to meet a lady whose
presence reflected the dazzling charlatanry
of her surroundings. He saw a white-haired,
brilliant-eyed woman with irresistible childlike hands and face. It was her face that
puzzled and set his brain at the leap.

Why did young lady specialists wear white
wigs? he asked himself. He was certain that
the natural hair beneath was a golden red or
brown. A woman, Tony argued, might build
up her age by the use of false hair, but the

eye of youth was difficult of concealment.
Madame Messonier's eyes were twenty years
old. By various tricks of toilette and the
costumier's art she had almost succeeded in
making herself a dowager in appearance.

Her glance passed from Hackett to Gifford
Renwick with unerring instinct.

"You desire to consult me?" She spoke
with her hand resting lightly on the back of a
revolving chair that tilted forward toward a
curiously designed retinoscope.

"Dr. Teroni Tsarka advised me to see you,"
Renwick answered quietly.

"Doctor Tsarka!" She repeated the name
as one trying to recall some long forgotten
personality. "It is so hard to remember these
names," she said at last. "People come and
go."

"Japanese nerve specialists are rare even
in London," he prompted. "Perhaps it does
not matter."

"Japanese!" She raised her hand from
the chair and smiled in recollection. "He
was badly burnt once through the bursting
of an over-heated bulb. It is very flattering
to be remembered by distinguished person-
alities."

"I shall remember you, madame, if I am ever again permitted to see the light." Renwick spoke with his face uplifted.

"You have been elsewhere?" Her eyes searched the blind face, the clear-cut features, the boyish mouth.

"To Sir Floyd Garston. He was not enthusiastic about my chances."

"One might as well go to the pyramids," she declared. At a sign from her Tony led Gifford to the chair, and, seating him carefully, retired to a respectful distance.

Renwick was conscious of a numbing pressure of the eyes as though a silver-rimmed ophthalmoscope were searching the cells of his brain. His nerves flinched under the strain. A needle of light seemed to probe and illumine the quivering depths of his retina. The light was withdrawn sharply. He heard her voice, and it sounded very far away.

"My fee is two hundred guineas. Your case would occupy several weeks — a month, perhaps. There would have to be extractions by a process of radiomagnetics."

Renwick half turned in the chair. "I — I

beg your pardon," he stammered. "Did you say guineas?"

"Two hundred," she affirmed coldly.

"I am not prepared to pay such an amount," was all he could say.

"Then I must wish you good-morning."

Stupefied by her words, he listened to the sound of her fast retreating steps on the carpet. Then, turning from his seat, called after her with a note of despair in his voice.

"If you think there is hope, I might raise the fee within a month, madame!"

"Do you think I would have asked if there had been none?" came sharply from the door.

"I beg your pardon, Madame Messonier. I merely desire to be frank with you. The sum is colossal — to me. But ——" He paused unsteadily, staring bleakly in her direction.

"You must not expect a miracle in ophthalmic surgery for half a guinea, Mr. Renwick," was her business-like retort. "Your case is not quite hopeless. You are suffering from radium poisoning."

She turned to Tony with a smile. "You may bring Mr. Renwick to me at any time within the next two days. After that," she paused, with a swift glance at the bent figure near the chair, "after that I cannot answer for the consequences."

The little detective drew a quick breath. "Two hundred guineas, madame. Pray consider," he urged with some feeling.

"I must wish you good-morning!"

She was gone, leaving Tony staring after her as she ascended the wide stairs leading to her private apartments.

"This specialist business beats all forms of gambling, Renny. It's money or your life with a vengeance. Lord, I thought there were a few angels in the medical profession! So far we've encountered nothing but blighters," he added under his breath.

The attendant showed them to the door with a frozen formality that jarred on Tony's nerves. To Gifford the situation was fraught with innumerable terrors. Something in Madame Messonier's brief examination convinced him of her knowedge and power. A charlatan would have bargained with him, would have accepted fifty guines before finally turning him adrift as incurable.

Never before had he felt how colossal were the barriers which separated the average man from two hundred guineas. In the past he had regarded such a sum as a mere trifle. Money-lenders were not all swindlers. And a young man occupying a fair position in the City might, under ordinary conditions, easily negotiate a loan of two or three hundred pounds at a moderate rate of interest.

In the face of Sir Floyd Garston's verdict, he could not ask his employer to assist in paying Madame Messonier's fee. Anthony Coleman would follow Sir Floyd's lead and insist upon his going to an infirmary. But just here Gifford felt an unutterable loathing at the prospect of an hospital ward. And there was something in his case that called for instant treatment.

Strangely enough Madame Messonier had diagnosed his symptoms of blindness in the precise terms which Teroni Tsarka had already made known to him. She had allowed him two days' grace wherein a cure was possible. It might be a trick to obtain money, he thought, but surely the directors of so magnificent an institute would hardly risk exposure as swindlers, or worse!

A drop of sweat fell from his brow as he stumbled into the car. "I must get that two

hundred," he panted. "Hartman & Isaacs
will let me have it at twenty. Tony, are you
listening? I must have the cash!"

"My dear Renny, Hartman & Isaacs won't
listen to you. Consider the facts. If this
eye trouble is permanent, how do you pro-
pose repaying them? They'll find out all
about your future prospects before they put
up a cent. No sar.e financiers ever advanced
money for the benefit of a quack specialist."

"Do you think that Madame Messonier
is that, Tony?"

"My dear boy, I saw her and you didn't.
She's an actress of the first magnitude. Bern-
hardt could not have bettered the part.
She's immense!"

Renwick flinche... "Can't you see how
she pounced on the real trouble. She said
distinctly that my nerves were suffering from
radium poisoning. She spoke of extracting
the poisonous matter by means of radio-
magnetics. In a word, half the London hospitals wouldn't know what she meant. Teroni
Tsarka said she would cure me. I believe him!"

"Bravo, Renny! Go home to-night and
sleep; I'll do my best to raise the money.
Will you go home?"

Gifford squirmed in his seat. He knew that the good-natured little man would sell or mortgage all his worldly possessions to help him. And Tony had a wife and family depending on his modest income.

"See here, Tony; don't bother about this affair. Now I come to think, there are some mining shares at home that were bought for me by Aunt Clara. They are worth more than two hundred at present prices. Funny I didn't remember them before."

Tony breathed a trifle easier at the news, although he marvelled why Gifford had never mentioned the mining shares before. At Waterloo station he provided himself with two tickets for Twickenham, where Renwick's widowed mother lived in a red-brick cottage near the river.

Arriving at the picturesque old town, they walked down a hedge-skirted lane where the early spring flowers peeped from moss-grown walls and garden rails.

A few sombre clouds drifted over the distant fields, yet, as they aproached the lane end, the sun rode from the piled-up masses, flooding field and highway with golden mists. Children's voices reached them from a near school-house. Everywhere, as they passed along, Gifford was assailed by a hundred familiar sounds that brought with them the memories of his childhood.

What a pitiable home-coming! Only a few days before he had followed the road to the station with the joy of life thrilling his senses. And now, by one of Fate's back-handed strokes, he was being led from place to place like a blind beggar.

Tony talked cheerfully, but his words fell dead on Gifford. Only two days remained wherein to obtain the money that would liberate him from the enveloping shades. Only two short days! In the silence that ran between heartbeats he told himself that his friend must not make sacrifices on his account. Tony had a meek-faced little wife, not over strong, and there were the children who would feel the bitter pinch if their father were permitted to engage in pecuniary liabilities on his behalf. After mature reflection on this point, Gifford felt glad that Tony had not questioned the story of the mining shares.

At the cottage-gate Hackett gripped his hand warmly. "Good-by, Renny. You'll hear from me shortly — to-morrow perhaps.

Keep your faith in Madame Messonier —
faith moves mountains."

He returned to the railway station feeling
that he had acted wisely in permitting mother
and son to meet alone.

Gifford fumbled at the garden-gate, which
had always opened at his lightest touch. A
voice was calling him from the ivy-burdened
porch, the voice which had crooned and
sung to him from his cradle and down the
years of his growing manhood. It touched
the roots of his nature now, as he stood listening, with head bent, in the garden path.

"Why, Gifford . . . What is the matter? You are home earlier than I expected!"

The white-haired mother came from the
porch quickly, but stayed a moment to consider the bent-shouldered son with the drawn
mouth and groping hands.

"Gifford! are you ill?"

He straightened himself instinctively at
her swift touch. "A bit of bad luck, mater."
His hand went up in sharp affirmation of his
words. "Got hit with a radio-active appliance. It's hard to explain. You see I was
conducting an inquiry."

He heard the quick breathing, felt the enfolding hands, and his mouth tightened painfully. "We'll go inside, mater. People won't understand if they see us here."

"Is it serious, Gifford?"

"Why, yes. The fact is I can't see anything. My employer wants me to go into an infirmary. There . . . mater; don't make a bad business worse!"

He held the sobbing figure tight in his arms. The darkness seemed very foolish to him now because, in spite of her enfolding arms, it separated him from the gray-haired mother. And he had never heard her cry before in this bleak, pitiful way.

"Mater," he said huskily, "we must not take it seriously. It is merely a question of two hundred guineas."

She led him into the cottage as a shepherdess leads a stricken sheep to the fold. Was this pain-drawn figure with the sightless face her son? It seemed incredible, monstrous!

The room appeared too small now for his searching fingers. He struck things in his efforts to find a chair. A glass shade fell with a startling crash as he put out an unwary hand.

"We'll have to get used to it, mater,"

he said, as his mother swept the broken pieces
together, "unless an angel from heaven comes
along with Madame Messonier's fee."

From his disconnected explanations Mrs.
Renwick grasped quickly enough the tragedy
of the situation. A lady specialist existed
whose skill and magic were only available
to the rich patients who visited her. All
the other London oculists counted for naught.
The two hundred guineas demanded was
more than she could ever hope to raise in her
lifetime, and her mind swept the financial
horizon for some shadow of hope that would
enable her to meet Madame's ruinous charges.

Gifford, his face resting between his hands,
broke upon her silent cogitations.

"If we sold and mortgaged everything we
own, mater, we'd never raise the money.
Yet if I neglect Madame's warning this
poison " — he touched his eyes briefly —
"will put me out of harness forever. If I
borrowed the money it could be repaid when
I returned to work. Hackett assured me that
the London financiers will not lend money to
sick men and women. The thing that hurts
most, mater," he paused, his face turned
to the gray afternoon light while his fingers

drummed the window pane uncertainly, "is the fact that I shall drag you and others down with me."

"Hush, dear; a way will surely open to us. If the worst comes, I will go to Madame Messonier and beg — ah, dear, you don't know the depths of a woman's heart. She will not let you perish. She is surely human . . . God has given her a soul and eyes to see even a widow's despair!"

Mrs. Renwick paused in her little outcry like a wounded doe crouching beside her offspring.

"She will listen, Gifford. She only saw you as a mere stripling. You did not appeal to her; you did not tell her what it all meant!"

Gifford was silent, his face pressed between his palms. He could not tell her that Madame Messonier was a business-like person steeled against the supplications of impecunious patients.

His fate, after all, was not in a woman's keeping; it depended upon the yea or nay of a Hebrew money-lender.

CHAPTER V

AFTER Gifford had left the Institute Madame Messonier retired along the white-panelled corridor to her own apartments. Opening the door of her private reception room she remained motionless, staring rather bleakly at an absurdly small figure reclining in a wide armchair.

"Doctor Tsarka!"

"Your servant, Beatrice. My Panhard car is almost as swift as the blind detective Renwick. You are not delighted to see me?"

Teroni Tsarka sat upright in the chair, nodding like a spring-fitted image. "What do you think of the priest-faced boy?" he asked softly.

"If you mean the young man who has just left the Institute, Doctor Tsarka, I may say that his case calls for speedy treatment. It is terrible to stand by and demand gold from the perishing!"

There were unshed tears in her eyes, a

quivering of the throat suggestive of grief restrained.

Teroni Tsarka studied her with a glint of amazement in his eyes. "I came here at a great risk to express sympathy with this Renwick, my dear Beatrice. By the merest accident he ran foul of my partner, Horubu, at a moment when he was conducting an experiment in the laboratory. Renwick entered my house without permission, and he must suffer the consequences."

Beatrice Messonier flushed to the temples. "I think your friend Horubu is little better than a coolie adventurer! He is too violent!"

"Renwick came upon us like a thief. We cannot permit these English detectives to violate the privacy of our home life. There is no need to pity Renwick. We must go on with our work, Beatrice Messonier. We must have clients — we must have money."

Doctor Tsarka fumbled with his gold-plated cigarette case, and permitted his feet to rest on the hassock beside him. Madame seemed unable to speak for a moment.

"I am your servant," she said at last. "But I warn you, Doctor Tsarka, against the inflexible nature of the rules which govern

this Institute. I will not play the vulture
on your behalf. Men and women shall not
go from here carrying despair and humiliation to their homes. Renwick is the first;
he shall be the last!"

There was no mistaking her vehemence.
Doctor Tsarka quailed a little. Then his
mouth seemed to tighten at the corners, his
small toes turned in like the paws of a wolf.

"You are not employed to think for me,"
he answered tartly. "And do not mistake
this Radium Institute for a benevolent asylum.
It was not inaugurated to cure the financially
distressed. We must have our fees; we must
pay our bills!"

Madame Messonier remained standing some
distance from him, her hand toying with the
lace of her sleeve.

"In six months I have been visited by three
patients, Doctor Tsarka. The first two came
out of curiosity to learn something of my
methods, the third departed a few minutes
ago, and, as far as I can judge, he may never
return. Being a woman, I am naturally
curious to know why you employ me with no
apparent profit to yourself or the company
you represent."

She turned to him almost wistfully, a pleading eagerness in her voice. "Pray take me into your confidence. Tell me why you retain my services as an oculist when people shun the Institute over which I preside, and the members of my own profession persist in regarding me as an unprincipled adventuress?"

The little Japanese doctor stared frigidly in her direction, then in a voice tinged with irony flashed back his answer.

"You have been provided with a princely residence, my dear Beatrice; your salary is paid regularly at each month end; yet, like most of your sex, you continue to ask questions. If man were to present womankind with the dome of heaven and the celestial wonders thrown in, they would contrive to ask questions. Tashan! I am very weary sometimes."

Beatrice Messonier had met the little Japanese doctor some two years before at the Tokyo University. He had presided over one of the life classes during her term, and he had been impressed by the almost superhuman skill displayed by her during an experiment in ophthalmic surgery.

Her undisguised interest in the new theory of Becquerel rays, as applied to the Japanese school of modern ophthalmics, had caught his fancy. Approaching her by degress, and with marked deference of manner, he discovered that the brilliant-eyed young student was a graduate from an American university. Her parents were settled in Los Angeles, and were of French descent. Imperceptibly, almost, Teroni Tsarka had imposed his strange theories upon her, theories which aimed solely at the regeneration of human thought as applied to the science of healing, until she sat at his feet, her young mind uplifted in the glamour of a new-found science.

It did not take him long to discover her genius for the study of ophthalmics. He marked her for his own among a score of English and American girl students. Where others brought their cloudy intellects to the unravelling of certain bewildering phases of natural phenomena, Beatrice Messonier saw with the eyes of a spirit child, divined with assimilated modern thought as though it were a food upon which her mind and soul grew strong.

Doctor Tsarka had a craftsman's regard

for the science of ophthalmics. To her it was a religion. He taught her the value of the Z ray, that weird offspring of radium which had provoked the ire and curiosity of German and English scientists west of Tokyo.

Tsarka had chosen her to carry out his scientific propaganda as a musician chooses a rare and beautiful violin. She responded to his lightest thought, echoed and refined his most abstruse utterances until they became a fixed law in the world of applied chemistry.

Leaving Tokyo at his suggestion, she had journeyed to London in company with a group of English and American girl students in the hope of obtaining a position in one of the city hospitals. Failure bleak and pitiless was the immediate result. Her American and Japanese diplomas were regarded with contumely by certain London house surgeons and hospital committees. Driven from place to place she had, at last, been compelled to seek a livelihood as a nurse in a public hydro, where bitter drudgery and officialdom stalked beside her for sixteen hours a day.

Then Doctor Tsarka, accompanied by his daughter Pepio, appeared in London, where many of the leading journals made haste to print copious extracts from his world-renowned pamphlet on "The Generative Sources of Radium."

Beatrice Messonier lost no time in communicating with her old instructor. She explained her ignominious position at the hydro, a fact which caused the little Japanese doctor an outburst of genuine anger. He said the English were experts in the art of bludgeoning the children of the gods. England had laughed at Darwin, had placed Napoleon to rot among the sea fowl at St. Helena, it had also turned the dear little child genius into a kitchen slave and a maker of poultices. There was no doubt whatever concerning the villainies of John Bull.

Beatrice throbbed when his letter reached her. How appreciative, how kind he was!

They met one evening on the steps of the Royal Institution, where he told her of his plans for erecting a Radium Institute for the benefit of wealthy incurables and the partially blind. Supporting him financially were half-a-dozen Japanese enthusiasts, who believed in the curative properties of his Z ray as applied to every form of human pain and disease.

Beatrice had listened to him with a heart that could not breathe. Here was her chance to prove herself in the eyes of a conservative medical profession. Here was a chance for the shy girl student who had burned brain and soul to acquire the secret of the god in the pitchblende. With her knowledge of radio-active substances everything was possible, the curing of the blind, the raising of the dead to life!

Within a month of their meeting, the building of the Radium Institute was begun, and Beatrice watched its completion with something of religious awe and veneration. Lastly when Doctor Tsarka, in token of his admiration for her splendid gifts, decided to add her name to its title, Beatrice felt that everlasting fame had been conferred upon her.

In the months that followed her installation as president of the Messonier Institute no patient had evinced a desire to undergo her system of treatment. The medical fraternity, in general, preferred to ignore her methods. Surprised at the unexpected turn of affairs, she had appealed to Doctor Tsarka, but that mysterious little man chose to smile at her impatience. The time was arriving, he pre-

dicted, when London would do her homage
and fill her consulting rooms with patients.

The months of waiting had failed to disturb his Eastern serenity. He laughed at
her fears, advised her to continue her experiments so that her hand might not lose its
cunning when the hour for its need arrived.

The ghostly silence of the Institute, unbroken through months of waiting, had
threatened to disturb the courage of Beatrice
Messonier. Of Doctor Tsarka's domestic affairs she knew little. He was a widower, with
one surviving daughter, Pepio, to whom he was
tenderly devoted. Only once had she visited
his city residence, upon which occasion she
had met several strange-looking boy students.
One man, Horubu, Doctor Tsarka's almost
inseparable companion, she detested at sight.
She was confident that Horubu was the
person who had assisted Tsarka to build the
Institute. He was a short-necked, bull-
headed man, with a powder blaze on his left
cheek. Always dressed in a frock coat and
silk hat, he impressed her as an ex-soldier seeking his fortune in England. Beatrice dis-
liked the undersized, unemotional Japanese.
For the life of her she could not rid her mind

of the idea that the Japanese, as a whole, suffered from arrested development. Of course, Teroni Tsarka was different.

The sudden appearance of Gifford Renwick had broken the spell of silence which threatened to demoralize the Institute. Yet with all her pity for the young detective's critical state she had been forced, in accordance with Tsarka's inflexible mandate, to demand her exorbitant fee.

"We are dealing in the most expensive curative substances known to science," he had warned her. "Patients will go to you only when driven by the fear of death or blindness. Maintain high fees. It is the best advertisement you can offer yourself."

So in lieu of her fee Renwick had been refused treatment. The thought stung her now as she gazed at her old instructor sprawling in the great velvet chair. To her the science of healing was a divine instinct, and her instincts clamoured for immediate freedom of action.

To have operated successfully on the young detective would have been her dearest wish. But she recognized her debt of gratitude to

Teroni Tsarka, together with her sworn responsibilities as director of the Messonier Institute. It was her duty, therefore, to adhere to the rules of his establishment.

He appeared to divine something of her thoughts as he lay back peering at her through half-closed lids. The turning away of Gifford Renwick from the Institute had hurt her he felt certain. Assuming an upright position his dozing eyes brightened curiously at the points.

"Do you think that Renwick is really incurable?" He made short stabs with his cigarette finger as if to emphasize his words.

Beatrice drew breath sharply as though drawn unexpectedly from the gulfs of self-analysis.

"The young man's case is serious. The iris is clouded with a spectrum of fire. You . . . know the cause," she ventured meaningly.

Doctor Tsarka bit his nails pensively.

"To put it technically, my dear pupil, the cornea received a bombardment of radioactive molecules. The work of extracting that poisonous luminescence is not difficult — for you."

"He may not come again," she pleaded.
"Let us —— "

He checked her with an uplifted forefinger
as he rose to pace the carpeted floor. "We
must keep up the fees. We must have high
prices for the use of our good brains. Only
fools give the result of their experiences
for nothing. Keep up the fees!"

He padded up and down the apartment, a
certain tigerish velocity in his movements.
Beatrice felt, as she watched, that his small
lithe figure held the pent-up vitality of a
nation. His boyish hand clasped a malacca
cane, and as he strode to and fro he made
little stabbing thrusts as one demolishing
unseen obstacles. He paused at last, in his
eccentric movements, and regarded her with
sudden interest. His tawny face seemed to
kindle with the fires of his brain.

"You have been very lonely in this" —
his cane circled the luxuriously appointed
room—"in this house of experiments. There
are times when you regard me as a mad fool
for investing money in its upkeep. Wait,
Beatrice Messonier. To-morrow, in a week
hence, the white light of fame shall enshrine
you. It shall beat upon your heart and brain;

you shall drink it like wine. Everything you shall have dreamt shall be yours. Princes shall come here to consult you; the lords, the queens of society will plead for a consultation!"

Beatrice stared at him, scarce believing her senses. His face had grown tender, the fierce lines born of overstudy and privations in the past gave way to one of unutterable serenity.

"The children of emperors shall come to you" he went on, "the statesmen and soldiers. You shall hear their voices in these rooms, and the news of their coming shall attract the nations!"

He spoke without a gesture or effort, and his words lost their flamboyance in the serenity of utterance. Only once did his clear voice jar on her senses. Its effect was quickly dispelled, however, by his trans-cendant manner.

"From boyhood I worked under the lash," he continued. "Poor, neglected, I grew to manhood with a desire in my heart to wreak a terrible retribution upon society. On every side I was met by greed and avarice even among my own countrymen. The feel-ing of anarchy left me as I grew older. With my brain harnessed for a conflict with the rich of England and America I struggled through the eighteen Gehennas of Mencius into the white light of Reason. And," he paused to moisten his lips, "in the name of Reason and Justice I have brought the weapon of science to bear upon the beast of sloth — the idle rich and the leering aristocrat."

Beatrice Messonier stared like one who heard the devils of science trumpeting through his speech. His small body swayed from side to side before he sank again into the wide, velvet-covered chair. The effort of speech had evidently fatigued him. Leaning over she touched his shoulder gently.

"You have always been good to me, Doctor Tsarka. I cannot forget that I was once a struggling student condemned to toil without profit to myself or others. Yet," she hesitated, with her hand on his swaying shoulder, "I confess that your motives are not very clear to me. How are these princelings and statesmen to be brought here? I do not understand."

"They will come because there will be no hope elsewhere. Beyond that I cannot tell you more. You must wait and trust me,

Beatrice Messonier. You have not toiled
and bled your wits for naught. Fame shall
wrap you in its everlasting garment."

"And you!" she cried, unable to resist his
fiery rhetoric. "What do you gain for your
labour and zeal?"

"Do not ask yet, Beatrice. This   . . .
outburst has wearied me. I think sometimes
of my little daughter Pepio. I would like
to see her happy, married to one of her own
countrymen."

He rose from the chair, staring dully at the
window that overlooked the street below.
"I must go, my dear Beatrice. You will
hear from me in a day or two." He stared
from the window into the street, his eyes
searching the forms of the passers-by as
though he dreaded venturing forth alone.

"My motor mask and coat are downstairs,"
he said slowly. "Let your attendant ring
up the nearest garage. I want a fast car to
take me some distance from town."

"Then you have left your late address?"

"Yes; the air was not good. There were
too many street noises, and the house itself
was undesirable. There were," he paused
an instant to wipe his heated brow, "rats in

it — those big, gray English rats that keep men awake."

After he had gone Beatrice Messonier sat near the window dazed and mystified by her benefactor's dazzling prophecies. Something in his manner suggested an approaching crisis in his own life and hers. What did his talk of princes and statesmen mean? She would have regarded such an outburst in another as the result of alcoholic excesses. But Teroni Tsarka was not given to the use of stimulants. He abhorred intemperance of mind and body. What he had spoken was the result of his structural philosophy, she felt certain. A tremendous crisis in medical research was at hand. And Teroni Tsarka was the man to sound the trumpet of science to an apathetic civilization.

CHAPTER VI

GIFFORD, with a sense of relief, retired to his room overlooking the garden. The odour of the fields, the smell of the wet grass and newly ploughed earth was balm to his radium-shattered nerves.

Madame Messonier had warned him of his approaching blindness. Upon this point her verdict had been clear and certain. The dancing pains had gone from his head, but in the still hours of midnight he became interested in the glossy red bulbs that floated across his retina. One by one these flaming discs rose like miniature suns before him, setting in celestial splendour into a sea of violet darkness.

In a little while the sea of violet became luminous with floating shafts of light, with here and there a dart of flame that resembled a gun flash.

Gifford felt instinctively that his optic nerves were experiencing the final colour storm which

precedes total blindness.   In the dawn he
prayed to be relieved from the scarlet horrors
that threatened to unseat his reason.   With
his drawn face to the waking day he invoked
the searing molecules of fire that flew imp-
like into the flowing Gehenna of sparks.
Millions of tiny light-pricks assaulted the
pupils of his eyes.   Invisible marksmen
fired into the white space where Reason sat,
until the furious enfilade of colour made him
cry out.

His mother entered the room, and, through
a volcano of down-pelting fire, he felt her
cool hands on his brow.

"You have not slept," she whispered.
"Is there much pain, dear?"

"As much as I deserve, mater.   Give me
a drink.   I've been through a storm of bursting comets.   And some of the bits struck
down!"

Mrs. Renwick held a glass of ice-cold water
to his lips, while he drank feverishly and
asked for more.   She noted a scared look in
his face, a look she had once seen in the face
of a burnt child.

"I've got another twenty hours before the
little red gods pass me out."   His hand

grasped the bed rail uncertainly, while a dryness seized his throat and lips.

"Do you know, mater," he went on, "that a Japanese scientist, named Tsarka, has discovered a real live god?"

"No, Gifford, I saw no mention of it in the papers," she answered soothingly. "Are they exhibiting it in London?"

Mrs. Renwick was certain that her son's mind had been distracted by his recent misfortune. "We had better call in Doctor Somers," she ventured cheerfully. "I'm sure he will do something for you."

"Somers is no use to me, mater. He doesn't know enough about my case to keep me cool. He'd give me a draught, probably, that would send me to sleep until morning, and the world would be a dead cinder to me when I awoke."

With his mother's help he dressed slowly, a grim sense of his position causing him to laugh woefully as he recalled his childhood days when the same careful hands attended to his immediate wants.

"I thought a man could lace his boots with his eyes shut, once," he said, his head bent to his knees. "But somehow the laces go wrong just as one's necktie refuses to lie straight."

"And where are you going with your tie so crooked?" Mrs. Renwick demanded wistfully.

"To town, mater, where I must beg, borrow, or steal Madame Messonier's two hundred guineas. She is the only person who has cornered the radium-god. She's got him at her finger ends and the little beggar jumps every time she whispers two hundred guineas!"

Gifford spoke from the bitterness of his soul depths, yet not without a touch of reverence for the woman who had diagnosed his case so skilfully. Mrs. Renwick's indignation at madame's exorbitant fee threatened to overcome his usual fortitude.

"I shall always think of madame as a heartless creature, Gifford. Why, the thought of suffering human nature ought to put the light of mercy in her eyes!"

"You don't understand these great specialists, mater. My case is one in a million. It may have cost her thousands of pounds to perfect her science. Think of the nights of study and experimental work she has had to go through. You can't blame her for demanding a high fee."

"It's cruel!" Mrs. Renwick declared passionately, "for a woman to withhold a cure when no other living person is capable of completing it.   Shame on her!"

Gifford made no reply as he groped from the room into the garden.   The sun was well above the dark poplars that fringed the distant meadows.   The warmth of spring leaped from the flower-strewn earth at his feet, tingling his young blood for a few brief moments, leaving him in the dark again. With a despairing gesture he spread out his hands to the sun-rays as one bidding adieu forever to the light of day.

Mrs. Renwick watched him striding with uncertain steps up and down the narrow path, past the white rose bush to the gate and back again.   Some children, passing on their way to school, paused to criticise the halting figure in the garden, the outstretched hands and pain-drawn features.

"He's playing a game," whispered a yellow-haired mite with a satchel.   "Blind man's buff or hide in the corner."

The sound of the childish voice reached

Gifford; he turned abruptly and entered the cottage, muttering under his breath.

"I must go to the money-lenders, mater," he said across the breakfast table. "I could repay them in two years."

"In two years," echoed Mrs. Renwick bleakly. "Imagine any creature on earth demanding two years of a man's life for a few days' work!"

"You are speaking of madame again, mater!"

"How can I help it, dear, when you have to go begging from door to door, from Jew to Jew, to obtain her iniquitous fee!"

"I shall go begging from door to door with a vengeance if the Jews are unrelenting. There's no employment in London for a blind man, mater. We'd better catch an early train to town. Each passing hour drags me nearer the pit."

The beauty of the spring morning filled him with a mad yearning to be out and doing. His heart clamoured for work and the sounds of the City. Inaction spelt death. Mrs. Renwick pressed a little food upon him, for she felt that the next few hours were going to decide his fate.

A familiar throbbing sound reached her through the half-open door, followed by the hoarse sob of a motor siren. Past the cottage it ran, and then stopped suddenly about twenty yards from the garden gate. Gifford, his senses strung to the snapping point, heard it shoot back and stop in front of the house.

Mrs. Renwick rose hastily from the breakfast table to peep through the window curtains. Her sudden exclamation of surprise roused her son from his reverie.!"

"Why, it's a Japanese lady; and she is coming up the path!"

Gifford was about to raise the cup of coffee at his elbow; he put it down sharply and stood up, his hand trembling against the table edge.

A tap, tap at the door prevented further speech between mother and son. Mrs. Renwick passed to the door and found herself staring into a pair of soft, brown eyes that peeped from the folds of an uplifted motor veil.

"I beg your pardon, madame; I was informed that Mr. Gifford Renwick lived here." The veil was thrown back now, and the brown eyes seemed to search the interior of the cottage.

Gifford's mother bowed slightly. "I am Mrs. Renwick. My son is at home, although hardly —— "

Her words were cut short by the appearance of Gifford in the passage. "It's Pepio Tsarka!" he said stonily. "Ask her what she wants."

His amazement at her visit was too profound to allow of further expressions of surprise. She spoke from the doorway, and he detected a sobbing undertone in her voice that jarred painfully.

"Oh, please listen, Mr. Renwick, and judge me afterward. I am so sorry; you know that we Japanese women are the tools of our men folk. It was your rashness that set Horubu to his dreadful task. Do not blame me."

"Well, what — what do you want?" he inquired flatly. "You have risked so much in coming here."

He could not overlook the fact that it was one of her people who had pressed the radium sponge over his eyes. What mad impulse had driven her to seek him out!

Acting on her own initiative, Mrs. Renwick drew the sobbing Pepio into the cottage, determined to find out why an apparently wealthy Japanese girl should seek out her son. Gifford stood awkwardly in the centre of the breakfast room, surprised and yet alert to catch the words that forced themselves from Pepio's lips.

"I have just left Madame Messonier," he heard her say, "that cruel America woman who dreams of nothing but English gold."

"Well," Gifford broke in impatiently, "has she consented to reduce her fee?"

"No, she will never do that. She is beyond all appeals to mercy. I came here to offer," she paused as though afraid of her own voice; "to offer the money she demands, because there is so little time left to restore the injuries inflicted upon you."

"You are very good." He spoke with his face to the window, a face which bore the blighting seal of her people's handiwork. "But I do not understand why you, of all people, should offer it to me, Miss Tsarka!"

Pepio quailed as though some one had struck her. A sense of his tragic dilemma was apparent in her tender eyes.

"Mr. Renwick, do not send me away without a hearing. Horubu acted for himself. My father scarcely anticipated his movements."

Leaning forward she touched his sleeve very gently. "Pray take this money, as a loan if you will, and try to think kindly of us."

"Thank you, Miss Tsarka, I have not yet descended to the taking of bribes from the man who stabbed me in both eyes," he cried fiercely.

"You are right," she admitted with a stifled sob. "Yet how could I have shielded you from Horubu's wrath. The same fate would have been mine had I attempted to warn you."

Gifford sought a chair, breathing sharply. Mrs. Renwick made violent signals across the table to the perplexed Japanese girl.

"Give me the cheque you have in your hand!" Her lips shaped the words only. "He will hear reason after a while."

Pepio slipped the cheque into her hand, and, with a swift glance of pity at the bowed figure in the chair, was about to withdraw. In the doorway she paused a moment, and then, with a frightened look in her eyes, returned hastily to the breakfast room.

"Some one is coming to the gate!" she whispered. A detective — a friend of your son's!"

She trembled violently as the garden gate opened with its unmistakable click, followed by heavy footsteps on the gravel walk.

"What do you mean?" Gifford rose instantly from his seat, his face to the door. Mrs. Renwick pivoted nimbly with a barely suppressed cry.

"It's Tony Hackett! What does he want, I wonder!"

"He is a detective!" Pepio insisted. "Please do not let him know of my presence. He might have me arrested. Pray allow me to go into another room while he is here!", she implored.

Her beseeching tones fell dead on Gifford. Once Hackett guessed her identity he would have her arrested instantly. Not for all the friendship in the world would Tony allow her presence in Renwick's house to plead her cause. Still ——

His mother pinched his arm.

"Gifford, be quiet. Let Tony pick up his own clues."

Without further parley she thrust the trembling Pepio into her bedroom and closed the door softly. Tony had halted in the garden to view the red-panelled car waiting in the road. He was a red-cheeked, middle-aged man with an alluring personality which had been responsible for the conviction of innumerable bank smashers and confidence men. Stooping in the path he examined with the air of a botanist the various shrubs that lined the well-kept flower beds.

Mrs. Renwick appeared at the door nodding serenely in his direction.

"You are out early this morning, Mr. Hackett! Gifford has only just finished breakfast."

Tony smelt the rose tree abstractedly before straightening his square shoulders.

"Thought I'd see how Gif was progressing. Had a bad night, I suppose?"

He shook hands deliberately with Mrs. Renwick, halted a moment in the doorway as though the presence of the red-panelled car, outside, had disturbed his equanimity.

He found Gifford seated near the window, his face sunk in his hands. A tense silence hung between them for a period of six heartbeats. Hackett touched the bent shoulder.

"Brace up, Gif, my boy. We'll be fit as a guardsman in a day or two. I've just been admiring the fancy car outside," he added cheerfully.

"It came to take him to Madame Messonier's," Mrs. Renwick interposed. "You would be doing him a service, Mr. Hackett, by accompanying him there."

Tony observed her from the corner of his swift eyes. "So the fee has been arranged?" he said, with an air of sudden surprise. "I thought perhaps there'd be some difficulty."

"Oh, we have a few friends remaining to us," Mrs. Renwick vouchsafed. "My son's trouble appealed to one of them at least."

Hackett's glance wandered from Mrs. Renwick to Gifford's downcast head. "I was ready to bet yesterday that only a wind from heaven could blow the money along. Well, it's a blessing, anyway, eh, Gif?"

Mrs. Renwick hurried outside and spoke in an unertone to Pepio's chauffeur. "Miss Tsarka has decided to stay until after lunch," she explained. "She desires that you should

take two gentlemen to town instead — to the
Messonier Institute, Huntingdon Street,"
she added, her memory racing back to the
address in Doctor Tsarka's letter which
Gifford had shown her.

The chauffeur nodded acquiescence. "I
get my fare in town, then?" was his only
question.

"When you return here with Mr. Renwick," she hastened to say; "he will come
back alone."

Gifford came from the cottage, and permitted Tony to assist him into the car.
While his mother kissed him she placed Pepio's
cheque for two hundred guineas in his coat
pocket.

"Don't let Hackett see Miss Tsarka's
signature," she whispered, as Tony leaned
forward to utter some final instructions to
the chauffeur.

Gifford writhed on the cushioned seat;
and in his agony he told himself that the fear
of blindness caused men to lose all sense of
honour and decency. Or how it came that he
had suffered the daughter of his enemy to
present him with a large sum of money?

He found little time to reproach himself,

for the car shot away at a good pace toward London. Tony's voice reached him indistinctly, but there was no mistaking its import.

"I picked up a scent where you broke off," he was saying. "Seeing that you are temporarily out of the running, Gif, I thought it a pity to let a good chance slip by."

Gifford nodded as he strained to catch each word. "Any arrests?" he queried huskily.

"Not yet. I found a chauffeur who used to drive Miss Pepio Tsarka about — the young lady who caused all your trouble."

Gifford shrugged in a non-committal way. "Go on," he said. "You'll find the Japs a pretty queer lot."

"This chauffeur," Tony went on, "was dismissed by Pepio for furious driving. I got nothing from him, even after I'd given him a half-crown, except the name and address of the driver who was in her service when last heard of. Well, I found driver number two's garage without trouble, and the number of his car," Tony continued, with merciless accuracy, "which, if my eyes serve me, Gif, is the number of the car we are riding in. Now, my boy," he placed his hand very quietly on his comrade's knee, "what on earth is the little game? How comes it that the daughter of Doctor Tsarka is allowed to hide in your house the moment I enter the gate?"

Hackett's words fell like a gunshot on Gifford. Only an expert of Tony's calibre could have connected the strands where he had let them fall. The name Tsarka, familiar enough to them both, had put the little detective on the trail of the nerve specialist's daughter. How he had unearthed Pepio's chauffeur was a piece of clue-hunting that would rank with his best work.

Gifford was thinking of his own position now. Hackett and he had been lifelong friends, assisting and advising each other during many trying periods of their lives, sacrificing at times their own personal interest for the other's welfare.

In the present instance Gifford felt himself squeezed between two iron walls. On the one side lay blindness, from which there was promised one way of escape — immediate treatment by the Messonier system of radio-magnetics and the payment of two hundred guineas. On the other, the forfeiture of his professional honour by the acceptance of money from one of a gang of Japanese adventurers.

He argued swiftly that the acceptance of the money was a matter of mere accident. To shield Pepio he had been forced to silence.

His head fell forward at the touch of his comrade's hand.

"Why didn't you tell me, Gif, that the cheque you're taking to Madame Messonier's is Tsarka's money. You see, it's so confoundedly awkward," Tony confessed, "for me to be hunting a pack of criminals while you, my dearest chum, are tactfully accepting their bribes!"

Gifford writhed under the lash of Tony's words. Yet he could not restrain the flood of anger that surged at the thought of his desperate condition. His nerves had suffered since Horubu had operated on him with his brain-searing devilries. It was causing him to sacrifice everything to save himself. Yet his sight was more precious than life itself. Without it he would drag through the remaining years in a pit of darkness, with only the sound of human voices around him — mere shadows mumbling across an eternal void.

He shrank slightly from his comrade's touch. "Tony," his voice was charged with the instinct of life, he breathed like one pressing through a tunnel where firedamp lay, "I'm going to get to the light that God gave to mankind. Don't force me back!" he cried fiercely. "I'll fight the devil himself before surrendering my last chance. You heard what Madame Messonier declared. Forty hours to save my sight; after that — hell!"

He spoke through his shut teeth, his hands thrust out like one pressing back the enfolding shades.

"Man alive, I'm not going to stop you!" Tony protested. "I only thought it a bit queer to find Tsarka's daughter in your house. It looks unprofessional, that's all, Gif."

"It does, but at present I don't give a brass farthing for my profession. I've been struck by a blast of lightning. And just when the world is advising me to retire to a blind asylum, the daughter of the enemy comes forth with the price of my resurrection!"

"H'm!" Tony sat back in the car twisting his watch chain irresolutely. "I'm not going to keep the light from a pal's eyes," he declared after a while. "All I can do is to sit quiet and see him through his inferno."

Five minutes later the car drew up at the Messonier Institute. Gifford alighted with Tony at his elbow, and together they ascended the steps leading to the white-panelled consulting rooms.

Tony spoke briefly to the liveried attendant. A wait of several minutes followed before he returned with the assurance that Madame Messonier would see Mr. Renwick immediately.

Gifford almost cowered in the interval of silence, a silence wherein the beating of Fate's wings was heard with each throb of his overburdened heart.

CHAPTER VII

SPRING peeped over the hedgerows with every budding flower and whitening rose. A noisy blackbird fluted insolently from a thatched eave where the robins had looked down on Gifford's window in the winter dawns. The midday sun warmed the wind-sheltered garden where Gifford plied his grass shears along the rose-bordered walks and lawn edges.

Mrs. Renwick passed up and down the path singing softly, as though the nearness of summer waked her slowing pulse and keened her interest in the life around her. Gifford's visits to the Messonier Institute were things of the past. The miracle in ophthalmic surgery had been accomplished in three short weeks, and Gifford, who had walked in the heart of a great darkness, was drawn by a woman's skill and magic from the pit where there is neither light nor the faces of human kind.

Sir Floyd Garston was the first to con-

gratulate him on the startling results of Beatrice Messonier's treatment. He had found
Gifford in a state of mental and physical
activity, and had confirmed, after a careful
examination of the young man's sight, the
absolute genuineness of the Messonier cure.

Sir Floyd had also visited the Radium
Institute, and had discovered that a coterie
of medical specialists had been before him.
Their cards remained on a silver tray near
the entrance hall. Sir Floyd felt a little
chagrin on learning that Madame Messonier
was not at home to members of her own profession. It was only fitting after her bitter
experiences at the hands of her professional
kinsmen that the brilliant Beatrice Messonier
should close her reception rooms to the men
who had refused her a hearing.

The "Renwick Miracle," as the medical
press chose to call it, had been singularly free
from after effects in the patient. When a
specialist of Sir Floyd Garston's calibre had
proclaimed the case hopeless it was time, the
critics asserted, that the potentialities of
madame's system became more widely known.

Gifford recalled the face of Beatrice Messonier as it appeared to him one morning,

when the mists of light penetrated the Stygian
darkness — a face ineffably serene and beautiful, out of which shone the pitying eyes of
a Christ-mother.

The light had leaped to her bidding, and
the fingers of her radium-gods had turned
back the engulfing shades. Gifford refused
to believe that the miracle had been accomplished by the aid of a moon-shaped disc
that revolved and gyrated before his naked
eyes. It was not the brain-pinching flow
of violet rays which had drawn the radium-
poison from the retina. Only her divine
power over mind and matter could have
accomplished the impossible.

His final visit to the Institute had oc-
casioned him many regrets. The loneliness
of the great white building, with its medley
of Christian and Pagan architecture, had
created in him a sense of religious awe. There
were stairways and apartments which bore
the impress of desuetude as of some ghostly
mansion inhabited by wraiths of the long
forgotten dead.

Who was she? he had asked himself a
hundred times. Who was this mysterious
child-woman, whose science and knowledge

made London's most honoured specialists
appear out of date and insignificant.

During the few short hours spent in the
operating chair she had never, by word or
sign, revealed to him the phases of her mind.
He had found her more mentally elusive than
a cloistered nun.

For weeks, after his cure, he had sought
only the green nerve-resting spaces which
surrounded his cottage home. He was like
one prepared to begin life anew. He had
not yet written to his employer in the City,
for there still lingered in his conscience the
memory of Pepio's two hundred guineas.
Until the money was repaid he could not
again follow the trail of the Japanese radium
thieves.

A letter came as he worked in the garden.
It was from Anthony Coleman, and briefly
worded:

DEAR MR. RENWICK : I feel it my duty to ask you to
return to your old position here. From experience gathered
in the past, we may look forward to more fortunate operations in the future.   ANTHONY COLEMAN.

Mrs. Renwick scanned the note with a
sigh of relief. "A kind, fatherly man for

all his brevity!" she exclaimed. "It will
give us a chance to repay Miss ——, er, I
really forget the Japanese lady's name. But
she had most expressive eyes."

"Um!" Gifford returned to the house
heavy browed and slow of foot. He was
certain that Coleman, of the International
Bureau, would not permit him to remain in
his service after what had happened. It was
an axiom that an official connected with any
branch of the detective service might not
accept bribes from criminals or their relatives.
He could never explain to Coleman's satisfaction the incident of Pepio's visit to his
house or the cheque for two hundred guineas.

Dressing with some precision, he ate a hasty
lunch and proceeded to the railway station.
Arriving in the City, he walked with secret
misgivings toward his employer's office.
Tony Hackett was absent from town, having
dropped the Moritz case in sheer disgust the
moment he learned of Pepio's action in ten-
dering the cheque for two hundred guineas
to his comrade.

Entering the Bureau, Gifford was greeted
with a hearty handshake by his chief. "Glad
to see you in town once more, Renwick,"

he affirmed with unusual affability. "When Sir Floyd made his report to us, we really thought your case hopeless. You did well," he continued, "in allowing Madame Messonier to operate; although Sir Floyd intimated very confidentially that you were assigning your guineas to a very superior charlatan. However, all that's changed, and we are glad to see you in harness again."

Gifford bowed his head in token of his employer's good wishes, and remembered Pepio's two hundred guineas. "I came here to tender my resignation," he began after a pause, "because you do not sympathize with a junior official who accepts a cash loan from the people he is commissioned to shadow!"

Anthony Coleman sat up in his chair. "What do you mean, Renwick?" he demanded quietly. "Are you speaking of yourself?"

Gifford nodded, while his face showed crimson in the afternoon light. His employer scrutinized him closely, a sudden hostility in his steel gray eyes.

"If you are referring to the Tsarka case, I may tell you at once that in accepting money from any of those Japanese adventurers you have violated the rules of the International Bureau. Bribery and corruption in you, Renwick, is — is unthinkable, outrageous!"

Anthony Coleman rose white to the lips, his tall figure quivering reed-like in his first gust of anger.

Gifford sat immovable in the chair, his fingers smoothed over his knee, yet his eyes responded to the flaming wrath of his employer, a response that held the unquenchable purpose of youth.

"A matter of two hundred guineas, sir. The young lady whom I had marked for arrest in connection with the Moritz affair was the giver."

"But the cheque; what did you do with it?" Coleman demanded. "In the name of heaven Renwick, can't you understand that you have compromised yourself with a school of swindlers, aided and abetted them to defeat the ends of justice! What became of the money?"

"Paid it to Madame Messonier," Gifford confessed. "You see," he paused to take breath for a moment, "I was faced by a proposition in which I stood to lose the sight of both eyes. Call it cowardice if you like, Mr.

Coleman, but in the end I surrendered my professional honour to save myself."

"You did not come to me."

"I had twelve hours to decide. Would you, Mr. Coleman, have been prepared to advance the money at so short a notice, and in the face of Sir Floyd Garston's report? Madame Messonier was in my estimation the only person in England capable of performing the miracle."

He rose and passed to the door slowly, knowing that he had forfeited a career which held the highest incentives to good work. There were other occupations open to him, but he could not help feeling that he was leaving the service a dishonoured man.

The steel gray eyes followed him to the door; the lips that were tight drawn as a pugilist's relaxed suddenly. Anthony Coleman gestured almost fiercely.

"Don't be a young donkey, Renwick. We do not employ men to go to the stake for us. If the Tsarka people are sufficiently conscientious to provide medical fees for which they are rightly responsible, it is no affair of ours. There are scores of wealthy criminals in this country ready to maim or cure their victims as the fit takes them. We must regard Doctor Tsarka's action as another of his eccentricities. It need not interfere with our future operation against him."

An electric bell rang at Coleman's elbow and continued furiously for nearly a minute. With his hand on the receiver, the head of the International Bureau bent forward to catch the message which had apparently disturbed the personal volition of the sender. Gifford noted the quick change in his employer's face as the words reached him, a look of frigid consternation that seemed to congest his features.

"One moment, Renwick." He spoke hoarsely, the receiver close to his ear. "The wildest thing has happened, a piece of lunatic comedy that will scare the wits out of the London public."

Then, as if by a preconcerted arrangement, the street became alive with screaming newsboys and men. The outer office door slammed violently. There came to Gifford the sound of voices in the passage, men calling excitedly to each other. Then the throbbing rush of a motor as it swept by from Scotland Yard in the direction of Westminster.

Anthony Coleman hung up the receiver and sat back in his chair. A grin threatened to relax the savage, tight-drawn mouth as he met Gifford's swift glance.

"We'll forget all about your resignation, Renwick," he said earnestly. "A strange thing has occurred at a little picture show in the West End that may afford you the chance of your life."

A messenger approached with a couple of evening papers, which he passed to the gray-haired chief seated near the telephone. A sharp glance at the scare-headed first page deepend the grin on this thin lips.

"Read!" He tossed the paper across the desk, and Gifford absorbed, in the shift of an eye, the sensational story printed beneath the lines of cross-headed matter:

"JAPANESE STUDIO INFAMY.

"SIX SOCIETY LEADERS TERRIBLY INJURED.

"This morning, while attending a small exhibition of pictures held at the rooms of the Japanese artist, Soto Inouyiti, several ladies and gentlemen received mysterious bodily injuries. Among them are the Duch-

ess of Marister, Prince Hohenhoff, and Mr.
Hardinge K. Hardinge, an American millionaire, and Baron Zillerstein.   It is well known
that Her Grace the Duchess of Marister
is a keen connoisseur of Japanese painting
and has, upon several occasions, induced her
society friends to accompany her to the
studio where Soto Inouyiti, a young and
talented artist, holds frequent exhibitions.
After a visit to the main salon the distinguished
visitors were conducted to the Scarlet Room
where Mr. Inouyiti has on view a microscopic
picture, in gold point, called the 'Haunted
Pagoda.' The picture was viewed at first
in the ordinary way, and then, at the suggestion of the artist, through a stereoscope
placed some distance from the picture.

"Her Grace the Duchess of Marister declared that, while gazing through the curiously arranged stereoscope, a sponge containing some electro or radio-active substance
shot down unexpectedly from an overhanging
shade, striking her over the eyes and causing
Her Grace intolerable pains. It is thought
that complete loss of sight may result.

"The case of the American millionaire,
Hardinge K. Hardinge, although less tragic,

is equally serious, for while seated comfort-
ably in a low saddlebag chair, a shower of
some chemically prepared solution was sprayed
over his face and head, with the result that the
hair and moustache of the genial American
have become a fixed purple.

"Equally serious is the case of Baron
Zillerstein, the well-known art patron. His
lordship, who is well past middle age and
inclined to corpulency, was caught in another
shower of radio-active molecules. Instead
of his hair becoming affected, as in the case
of Mr. Hardinge, his lordship's skin has been
covered with a multitude of dark spots.

"These dark spots have caused the Baron
great annoyance of mind. Immediately after
the depressing incidents mentioned above his
lordship adjourned in great haste to the
nearest swimming bath. But even after
the most copious ablutions, combined with
hot geyser baths, the spots remained.

"A specialist, who visited the Baron this
morning, declares that the spots are ine-
radicable until some one invents a process
for extracting radium molecules from the
pores. His lordship has therefore refused
to appear in public.

"The whereabouts of Soto Inouyiti," the article concluded, "are unknown. He is said to have left the studio immediately after the outrage."

Anthony Coleman glanced inquiringly at Gifford. "This affair is wholly Japanese. The blinding of the Duchess of Marister suggests your own experience with that rascal, Doctor Tsarka. What do you think?"

Gifford was not inclined to venture an opinion until he had visited the scene of the outrage. That the artist, Soto Inouyiti, was one of Doctor Tsarka's intimates he was well aware. He had met the handsome boy artist, in company with Pepio, only a few months before. Summarized from the newspaper report, the crime appeared motiveless, chaotic, for what could the Japanese gang expect to gain by such a fantastical outrage?

Coleman fidgeted uneasily. "If this last iniquity passes without a conviction we, as well as Scotland Yard, will have to reorganize our methods. And Prince Hohenhoff's friends have asked us to investigate."

"I'm afraid that these Japs are laughing at us," Gifford responded. "Doctor Tsarka jeers at what he terms our lack of imagination."

"The scoundrel!" burst from Coleman. "He and his associates appear to have discovered a destroyer of human energy in radium. Personally, I fear that we shall find ourselves unable to cope with this new school of Asiatic criminals who regard the blinding of men and women as a pleasant pastime."

He accompanied Gifford to the door and remained silent for a while as though listening to the cries of the passing newsboys. Then, through his shut teeth, uttered his final word of advice:

"You've been in Tsarka's clutches, Renwick, and I recommend you to treat him to a period of penal servitude just to wipe off old scores. The case is in your hands. Don't fail us this time. Good-by!"

CHAPTER VIII

GIFFORD pondered swiftly as he hurried in the direction of the studio where Soto Inouyiti had held his inhuman carnival. The studio was a three-story building of unpretentious appearance, and had been rented by the Japanese artist some months before. It was from the lift boy that Gifford gathered many unreported minor incidents. Quickness of perception is not the ruling passion among London lift boys, but it has often developed under the influence of a silver tip.

The boy, his face luminous with information, pocketed Gifford's half-a-crown in a way that won the young detective's instant admiration. "You see, sir," he began in breathless haste, "quite a lot of ladies and gents 'ave dropped in here lately to see Mr. Innerwitty's colour work. I may say there's been a hextra rush of barons an' millionaires in the last two days.

"This mornin' Mr. Innerwitty gave a

special show to a little crowd of real swells. I was up on the second floor givin' the care-taker a 'and with the plush carpet. Mr. Innerwitty (you see, sir, he's only what you call a boy), he tips me half a "sov." just to show Her Grace the Duchess to the proper door when her carriage stopped outside."

"Were there any Japanese attendants be-side Inouyiti?" Gifford questioned.

"No, sir. It was what you'd call a one-man show. I opened the door an' the artist did the salaamin'. I forgot to mention that he was dressed in white, sir; kind of naval ducks with a red tie flyin' loose from his collar, an' a funny green stone ring on his middle finger."

The lift boy paused to grin expansively at the memory of the initial proceedings.

"Mr. Innerwitty performed a kind of cake-walk, sir, when the Duchess trooped in an' said a few kind words about the spontaneous combustion of his sunset colourings."

Gifford suppressed a laugh at the boy's mimicry of certain art critics who had evi-dently visited the studio. "Go on," he said. "I want to hear more of the Baron."

"Well, sir, the show went off all right until

the party adjourned to the Scarlet Room, where the 'Haunted Pagoda' was hung. The Jap advised the ladies to see the picture through a sort of magnifying glass. The picture wasn't no bigger than a saucer; it had a big gold frame though, and gave you a kind of Weary Willy feelin' when you looked at the pagoda where the Japanese spirits were supposed to live.

"I must say, sir, the talk in the studio was elevatin'. Baron Sillystein grunted like a hippo when he spotted it.

"'Id was a lot too smalls,' he says to Mr. Innerwitty. 'A thousand pounds vas too much for a ting you can put in your vaistcoat pocket!'

"The Jap did a salamander bow, an' his scarlet tie flapped like a parrot's wing, sir.

"'The "Haunted Pagoda" is my life's work,' he says to the Duchess. 'It is a flame in colour. You look once at it an' see only the colour. You look again an' behold the living art of Soto Innerwitty. You look again, and lo, there comes to you the white fear of old Japan, fear of the departed spirits, the cryin' of our trees, the voices of the forest, and the heartbeats of our mountains.'

"Yes, sir, that's the kind of stuff he reeled off to the company. I got it all pat, because I'd heard him sling it at those newspaper chaps that used to drop in.

"Well, the Duchess had a peep through the stereoscope thing, while the Baron dropped into a chair close by, fannin' himself with one of Mr. Innerwitty's big palm leaves.

"Now, sir, I'm tellin' you just what happened, because I was standin' by the red screen near the door — waitin' for orders. Mr. Innerwitty slipped out of the studio an' went into a little closet at the back, where he'd fixed up a lot of wires an' insulators to connect with the studio.

"Standin' behind the red screen, sir, I spotted a kind of blue flicker pass over the stereoscope where the Duchess was peepin' at the picture. Then a small copper fan started to whizz just over Mr. Hardinge's head, and another over the Baron's. At first I thought it was a new kind of spring machine for keepin' people cool. But the Baron didn't think so. He gave a yell that had a German swear word wrapped in it. He landed in the middle of the studio on all fours, screamin' out that some one had emptied a pickle jar over his face. He could feel the stuff burnin' holes in his clothes, he said.

"Mr. Hardinge was in a similar fix, sir. The spray got in his hair an' turned it the colour of the pagoda. He was very quiet, Mr. Hardinge was, and went to the assistance of Prince 'Owenoff and the Duchess.

"Her Grace was almost cryin', sir. I found her sittin' on a couch wipin' her eyes. Prince 'Owenoff had just come away from the peep show an' was doin' the same."

Hereat the lift boy breathed like one who had witnessed the most startling crime in the century. "That's how things were," he continued, "when Miss Violet Cranstone came into the studio, sir."

"Do you mean Miss Cranstone the comedy actress?" Gifford questioned.

"Yes, sir, the one that's got her picture on all the post-cards. Mr. Innerwitty is supposed to be engaged to marry her. She's rather pretty, sir, if I may mention it."

"Go on," Gifford nodded impatiently. "What was Miss Cranstone doing in the studio at such a time?"

"Nobody can say, sir. All I know is that she walked straight to the stereoscope

and took a free peep at the 'Haunted Pagoda.'
When I called to her, sir, she was rubbin' her
eyes just like Prince 'Owenoff an' the Duchess.

"What with the Baron roarin' for swimmin'
baths, an' the ladies callin' to each other,
the studio was a little pandermonium, sir.
I telephoned very prompt for the police, an'
we had a couple of doctors here in no time.
The Duchess went away in the Prince's car,
while the other ladies were sent to their homes
by the doctors.   The last I saw of the Baron
he was on his way to a private swimming
bath."

Gifford followed the lift boy into the studio,
and found it occupied by a group of reporters
all bent on solving the mystery of the phe-
nomenal outrage.

Many of the pictures, including the "Haunted Pagoda," had been removed.   Gifford
learned that a foreign-looking man with a
hand-barrow had taken them away only a
few minutes before the arrival of the police.
A visit to the second floor atelier revealed a
number of small oil paintings, together with
a tangled coil of magnesium wires at the
stair head.

The voices of the reporters rose and fell

as they compared notes, each seeking to attach some real meaning to the Japanese boy artist's crime. He had not sought by threats to squeeze money from his distinguished visitors. They had come to see his pictures with a view to their ultimate purchase. Yet, at a moment when the wealthy Duchess of Marister had evinced a desire to possess one or more of his works, the young artist had deliberately set himself out to blind and injure his well-disposed patrons.

What were his motives? The press men retired in a body, leaving the mystery of Inouyiti's conduct still unsolved. Gifford, as he leaned over the bannisters, was suddenly conscious of a tall, red-faced woman waiting at the studio door below. She was dressed in a faded gray ulster, and her eyes appeared to be searching every corner of the apartment.

"Is Mr. Inouyiti in?" she demanded in a high-pitched voice. "Will some one tell him that Mrs. McGuire is here?"

The sound of her voice reached Gifford with startling force. In a flash he remembered her as the charwoman who had released him from Doctor Tsarka's house after the little nerve specialist had left him blind and half-drugged in the sleeping room adjoining the laboratory.

He descended the atelier stairs without a sound, and confronted her suddenly. "Excuse me," he began briskly. "I think we have met before!"

Her face crimsoned at sight of him. With an easy laugh she appeared to recover her ready self-possession.

"Sure I never met ye before," she declared. "I'm entirely a stranger to this part of the town."

"At Doctor Tsarka's," he prompted. "The morning you came to clean the empty house. I think you understand."

A look of blank annoyance crossed the Irishwoman's face.

"I've no remembrance of the circumstance, or I'd be admittin' it," she replied with assumed unconcern.

"You appear to be on hand whenever a member of the Tsarka family deserts a house or studio," Gifford alleged. "You are not telling the truth."

Hereat the charwoman broke into a torrent of explanations in which she invoked the earth and sky to witness the truth of her first and only statement.

Gifford's manner changed swiftly. The fortunes of his chief, his own future, depended on the speedy solution of the Inouyiti crime. The woman knew something and was trusting that his recent blindness would prevent his identifying her.

Approaching the telephone in the passage he made an adroit pretence of ringing up Scotland Yard.

"Please send a man to the Inouyiti Atelier, Cumberland Place." He spoke into the receiver sharply, clearly. "There's a person here I want to have arrested."

The charwoman trembled violently, and then broke into tears as he proceeded to lock the passage door.

"I'll be honest, sorr, an' spake the whole truth if ye'll spare a silly owld woman the shame of goin' to gaol."

"Who sent you here?" Gifford demanded. "Speak quickly, or you may regret the consequences."

"'Twas Mister Inouyiti that implored me to go to the first floor room, sorr. 'Tis only a boy, he is, an' sorry I was to see him in such trouble."

Her voice broke into a painful whimper; tears coursed down her scarred cheeks. "Don't sind me to the lock-up, sorr. I'm owld an' wicked, but not a thief; oh, not a thief, sorr!"

"Go on. Did you come here for papers left behind, letters or instruments of any kind?"

"No, sorr," she sobbed heavily, wiping her cheek with a big red kerchief. "The little Japanese gintleman left one av his fingers on the first floor. 'Twas caused by a wire twistin' sudden an' causin' it to tear at the joint."

Gifford smiled astutely. "Come, my good woman, you must speak the truth. These silly inventions will not serve you."

"'Twas not Inouyiti's real finger, sorr," she protested tearfully. "Only one av those rubber inventions he wore in public. A thing wut a little spring inside. 'Twill be somewhere about the room, I've no doubt, sorr. The finding' av it will prove the thruth av my words."

Gifford pondered briefly, and then, with the zest of a twelve-year-old boy, began a swift investigation of the studio. The Continental Police might assist in solving Doctor Tsarka's

inscrutable operations once he could prove
that a four-fingered boy artist was the leading
mover in the gang. He was confident now
that the Japs were working with the assistance of foreign emissaries.

A cry from the charwoman took him
across the studio with a bound. She was
stooping beside a bust of a samurai warrior,
a small flesh-coloured digit in her hand.

"Give it to me!" he said quietly, "and
please remain where you are for a moment."

Gifford repressed a cry of wonder as he
examined the little rubber contrivance which
Inouyiti had worn in public. Flexible as
elastic, it was modelled with considerable
delicacy. Jointed at the butt with lip-
shaped spring, it proved on examination to
be as tenacious as a real finger. Gifford
realized in that moment something of the
matchless art which enables Japanese criminals to avoid the snares of European and
American police.

The duplicate finger had evidently been
dropped by the artist in his wild haste to
leave the studio the moment his victims had
become aware of the infamous trap into which
they had been decoyed.

A sharp cross-examination of the char-woman elicted nothing further than the fact that she had been frequently engaged by Doctor Tsarka as a messenger and house-help. Gifford's lips tightened.

"How did Inouyiti communicate with you when he discovered that he had left this behind?" He held up the rubber finger insinuatingly.

The charwoman answered his question without a blush.

"'There's a tiliphone in the house where I lodge, sorr. 'Tis kept by a couple of nurses. Whinever the docthor or Mr. Inouyiti wanted me to clane up the place they just rang for me."

Gifford placed the finger in his waistcoat pocket, confident that the boy artist could be more easily traced than his more astute *confrère*, Doctor Tsarka.

The charwoman gave the name of Rose McGuire, and Gifford, after an exhaustive search of the studio, decided to allow her to return home. He was careful, however, to place a couple of smart men near the house in the hope that Inouyiti might show himself before night.

In the streets he was met by hosts of flaring posters on the hoardings. Some of these referred to the outrage as The Spotted Baron and the Blue-whiskered Millionaire. Others assumed a more serious note, while the majority dwelt upon Miss Violet Cranstone's untimely entry into the studio.

It occurred to him that a visit to the house of the famous comedy actress might cast more light on the affair. While doubting the story of Inouyiti's attachment for Miss Cranstone, Gifford felt that the unforeseen tragedy might eventually draw the little artist in her direction. He was certain, however, that Inouyiti had never intended to injure her in any way.

An evening paper supplied him with Miss Cranstone's address in South Kensington. A sharp walk in that direction helped to clear his mind, and he wondered, as his eye sought the number among the rows of semi-aristocratic houses, whether the inevitable batch of reporters would be in attendance.

A smart servant answered the bell. Inside he was met by a white-haired lady in black, who assured him almost instantly that her daughter had been the victim of a wicked conspiracy.

Gifford's card bearing the impress of the International Inquiry Bureau paved the way to Mrs. Cranstone's confidence.

Her daughter was at that moment in her room awaiting the coming of a second oculist who had been called in to examine her radium-scarred eyes. The first one, a well-known London specialist, had proclaimed her case hopeless. The nerve trunk had been destroyed, he asserted, by a powerful infusion of some radio-active material.

Gifford listened attentively to Mrs. Cranstone's story of her daughter's visit to Inouyiti's studio. Violet had gone there in the hope of seeing the "Haunted Pagoda." It was perfectly true that the Japanese artist had become violently enamoured of her daughter, and had visited their home upon several occasions.

Gifford followed Mrs. Cranstone into a small apartment where only a single light burned. On a couch, her face slightly exposed, reclined a young lady of eighteen or nineteen years of age. Gifford felt the white terror palpitating through her nerves, for he himself had endured similar torment when Horubu's radium sponge had almost pressed the light of reason from his mind.

But even through the terror which set her trembling at each unexpected sound Gifford was conscious of the subtle beauty of her English face. She lay very still, like a half-crushed flower, bruised and shaken after a fierce blast of wind.

He sat near her, scarce daring to break the silence, a silence he had felt when the radium devils were dancing through his brain. She was crying very softly, as though unaware of a strange presence, and each quick sob touched him with its breath of tragedy.

Mrs. Cranstone spoke, her hands resting near her daughter's.

"It has made us feel the need of a stronger power, Mr. Renwick. This morning when Violet left the house I felt that God had given the day for her alone. We mothers are weak and selfish; we are proud of our children's talents or beauty. Then the lightning comes, and we are ashes. Look at my daughter!"

Gifford had experienced many pathetic scenes when interviewing various classes of victimized citizens, but nothing touched him so sharply as the white-lipped despair of the radium-blighted comedy actress.

The sound of her mother's voice drew Miss

Cranstone from her trance-like stupor. Her hands were clenched in the cushions as though from the stinging flashes of light that stabbed the darkness around her.

"I cannot bear this agony much longer, mother. At first it was only a film of colour, now it is a wheel of fire, a torment of violet rays."

Gifford vouchsafed to address her without permitting his voice to jar on her radium tortured senses. He told her how he had fallen into the hands of Japanese nerve-scientists, and of his temporary blindness, followed by hours of unspeakable colour delirium until Beatrice Messonier had dispelled the darkness and the pain with the magic of her art and science.

Miss Cranstone listened to him as he described his partial blindness, the night of horror experienced when the Dantesque colour wheels flooded his nerve centres with a whirlwind of white fire.

"Yet to-day I am well enough," he said consolingly. "And, although my mission here is not to recommend a choice of doctors, I cannot allow my own experiences to pass without volunteering a word in favour of the Messonier Institute."

Mrs. Cranstone was deeply impressed by Gifford's words, and was barely restrained from communicating instantly with Beatrice Messonier.

Violet Cranstone lay quite still on the couch, hope thrilling her like a sweet narcotic. Yet Gifford divined by the sudden facial tremors that the colour-fiends were stabbing her with javelins of red and white.

Mrs. Cranstone held her tight as though her own pulsing heart could stem the cataracts of flame that swirled and flowed before her daughter's sightless face. And Gifford saw that the mother's lips prayed instinctively, just as the mothers of old prayed when the fiery terror leaped from the mountain side to engulf their children.

Like Gifford's mother, Mrs. Cranstone was a widow, and depended upon her daughter's efforts in her struggle to maintain her position in life. Violet's salary, although not large, had sufficed to tide them over the most trying period of their existence. It seemed like one of Fate's savage ironies that Violet Cranstone should have entered the studio at a moment when Inouyiti's lunatic schemes were in course of operation.

Gifford sighed as he contemplated mother and daughter.

A ringing of the electric bell aroused him from his brief depression of spirits. The servant entered softly to announce Sir Floyd Garston. Gifford rose instantly from his chair and after a hasty apology to Mrs. Cranstone, withdrew.

In the hall he was met by the famous oculist. Sir Floyd's hand sought his arm inquiringly.

"Good evening, Mr. Renwick!" he exclaimed cheerfully. "This radium business has brought us together again. Rather funny, eh?"

Gifford, in his mental abstraction, made casual reference to the dullness of the afternoon, and was about to depart. Sir Floyd's hand again detained him.

"Your advice in this matter may be of inestimable service to me and others, Mr. Renwick. I should be glad of a few moments' conversation after I have examined Miss Cranstone."

Gifford waited in the hall while the old physician hurried in to the terror-stricken young lady and her mother. Sir Floyd's staccato voice reached him from time to

time, and to the young detective the examination appeared pathetically brief.

The door opened after a while and Gifford,
marvelling at Sir Floyd's sudden outburst
of confidence, accompanied him to the carriage outside.

"Get in!" Sir Floyd commanded cheerfully. "I want to talk to you above all men,
Mr. Renwick; for I honestly believe that you
are the only person who has survived this
new offspring of the modern laboratory."

Gifford nodded as one prepared to listen
to an important statement.

"It becomes me," Sir Floyd went on, "as
a dutiful servant of the old and new elements,
to confess my inability to treat or even
diagnose correctly this painful affliction in-
vented by a gang of Japanese lunatics."

"Science moves, sir," was all that Gifford
could volunteer.

"It leaps, my dear Mr. Renwick; it leaps
and leaves some of us gasping in the dark.
For thirty years I have received measures of
appreciation from the highest in the land.
And . . . like all great artists, have been
content to bask in the light of a well-earned
reputation. With the flight of the years my

interest in research work has decreased. The advent of Curie has left me only partially enthralled. I have regarded the god in the pitchblende as a mere discovery, not a revolution."

The carriage ambled in the wake of the swift motor traffic, a circumstance which appeared to Gifford as symbolical of the slow-thinking physician seated beside him— the once renowned ophthalmist who had permitted the new scientific movement to pass and leave him grumbling in the rear.

"There are three radium specialists in the world to-day," Sir Floyd continued. "Laban Steiglitz of Berlin; Emile Roche of the Paris Institute and," he gestured impatiently, "our own Beatrice Messonier."

"May we assume that she is Steiglitz's equal?" Gifford ventured.

"She is more. The German has method and a genuine passion for research. Beatrice Messonier has the Christ-gift that is above art and study, just as the Nazarene's powers were above the doctors of Judea. So . . ." he brooded a little before completing the sentence, as though each syllable were a coin .of value, "so there was nothing left but to advise the Duchess of Marister and Prince Hohenhoff to consult Madame Messonier at once."

Gifford looked up in surprise. "Did you advise Miss Cranstone also?" he asked.

"Emphatically. Even an ultra-conservative like myself dare not risk the life vision of an aristocratic clientele. For one who has been late in the race," he added with an affectation of blitheness, "there is always the joy of hailing the swift. Beatrice Messonier deserves her triumph. She thundered at the gates of science where I merely tapped."

Gifford experienced a measure of relief now that Miss Cranstone's case was in the hands of Beatrice Messonier. He could not help wondering, however, what strange humour had led Sir Floyd into so candid a confession of failure. It was unlike the average medical man, he thought, to laud the students of the new school of radium therapy.

Arriving at Trafalgar Square, he alighted from the carriage after shaking hands with the old physician.

"I have done with my profession, Mr. Renwick," he said from the carriage window. "But before retiring I should like to ask the

Scotland Yard officials, and the International Inquiry Bureau in particular, what they are doing to prevent an organized band of Japanese miscreants from paralyzing the wealthy art patrons of Great Britain!"

Without waiting for an answer Sir Floyd signalled the coachman to drive on.

That evening Gifford dined at a Bohemian restaurant in Soho, where he had first encountered the laughing-eyed Pepio Tsarka. He felt certain that the little Jap doctor would never permit her to venture abroad again unless under cover of a fast travelling motor-car.

Dinner over, Gifford took out his note-book, intending to jot down a few impressions of the studio outrage. His pencil lay inside his vest pocket, and as he drew it upward he discovered that the rubber finger obstructed its egress. With some care and patience he separated them from the pocket lining, and as he was about to replace the rubber digit his eye caught a faint emission of light which seemed to radiate from the hollow inside.

Probing it gently with the pencil point, he noted that the light emissions increased in duration and power. Holding the finger beneath the table-cloth, he was astonished at the volcano of violet rays that illumined the dark space below.

"Why, the infernal thing is radio-active!" he gasped.

A thrill of terror ran through him as he held it below the restaurant table. Like a child who had experienced the horrors of radium blindness, he regarded the luminescent flow of light with a beating heart and tight-clenched lips.

CHAPTER IX

I F THE gods did not invent motor masks,
they blew up the dust that makes men
wear them."

From his study window Doctor Tsarka
commanded a view of the river where the
swart barges moved in sullen procession
toward the smoke-bound city. A thick-set
Jap sat in the shadow of the heavy window
curtains, his head sunk forward on his chest.
On a table in the centre of the room lay a
pair of motor masks and leather-lined travelling coats.

Abandoning his City residence the morning
after Gifford's entry, Doctor Tsarka had
sought refuge in Horubu's house at Purfew-
on-Thames. There was little to fear now
from the radium-stricken detective or his
confrères; for by the time Gifford had regained sight Teroni Tsarka hoped to be in a
position to defy the unofficial hirelings of
the International Inquiry Bureau.

Doctor Tsarka was scanning a road map,

his back half-turned to his companion, his great brow creased in thought.

"These English detectives do not worry us much, Horubu," he said without a glance from the map. "In Nippon we should have been strangled for our efforts."

"The man Renwick is the only one we have to fear."

Horubu spoke in a tight wheezing voice, interrupted by a violent fit of coughing that left him gasping like a fever patient in the chair.

Doctor Tsarka leaned forward to pat him between the shoulders until the paroxysm ceased.

"Your cough has an echo, Horubu." He peered into the flat, black-toothed face in the chair almost affectionately. "I have known the New York police to identify a man by his cough."

"This river fog is my poison," Horubu admitted gruffly. "I will return to Nagasaki in the summer. Our radium schemes work slowly, Teroni. We grow old."

"And rich," Tsarka chuckled. "This week will see the British gold pouring into our hands. Not for naught have we used our good brains. To-day is the one chosen for Inouyiti's assault on some of the British and foreign aristocracy. Eleven o'clock was the hour. There is an American gold-dollar man, a prince, a duchess, and a beefy German baron to be dealt with."

"German barons are poor game," Horubu grumbled. "They taught us economy. Why did not Inouyiti draw in a few more rich Americans?"

"The boy did his best. He is very clever."

"He talks too much." Horubu grimaced from the curtain folds. "These artists have the tongues of women!"

Tsarka nodded thoughtfully. "He is in love with an English actress, a girl of the Cranstone name."

Horubu sat forward breathing slightly.

"But Pepio, your daughter," he ventured. "I thought there had been a marriage contract! Pepio would have made Inouyiti a good wife."

Doctor Tsarka laughed lightly.

"I do not value the connection, Horubu. He is a slender boy of no particular family, no physique. Yet I feel that he has slighted Pepio."

"You love your daughter." Horubu inclined his bullet head in token of respect. "A good daughter, a good wife."

"She is the last of my house," Doctor Tsarka declared. "I am a busy man; yet there are times when I pause at my work to think of her, Horubu. A little while ago she was a prattling baby. To-day she is studying English art and letters. I think Inouyiti has slighted her for this fair English actress. Still, we must bear with him. Listen!"

The sound of a motor-car entering the street reached them. Ten seconds later they heard a key fumbling in the lock; footsteps wild and uncertain blundered down the entrance hall before the study door was flung ajar. Inouyiti, his red necktie fluttering beneath his passion-lined face, entered; his burning eyes turned upon the lean figure of Doctor Tsarka.

"The work is done!" he panted. "Give me a drink. I am sick; my head is full of pains. Oh . . . Tsarka!"

He reeled across the study, clutching at the table-edge to steady his shaking limbs.

The little nerve specialist pressed a glass

of spirits to his lips, a flush of anticipation lighting his own dark features.

Horubu scowled at the young artist's manner of entry, the flaring red necktie, the loose coat and stammering speech. Asoya Horubu had seen service with General Oyama during the bitter campaign in Manchuria, and his soldierly instincts revolted at Inouyiti's hysterical behaviour.

The brandy steadied the young artist; his breathing became more regular, his manner less distracted. Doctor Tsarka stooped toward a shaded lamp at his elbow and lit it carefully.

"We rejoice to hear that you have operated without mishap, Inouyiti." He glanced upward at the boy artist, his dark face illumined in the lamp glow. "Horubu and I salaam to your initiative and dispatch."

Inouyiti quailed in his seat. "There has been a mistake!" he broke out. "I was powerless to prevent it. Some devil of mischance has shattered my dream of happiness. Woe! I suffer! Only death will expiate my blunder. Help me, Teroni Tsarka, to bring about my end!"

He flung out his arms in passionate despair

as he sought to cover his face from Horubu's menacing eyes. "I am sick of life. Help me, Tsarka, to end it!"

His loud sobbing brought a snarl from Horubu. Rising, the old war veteran was about to leave the study, anger and disgust in his battle-scarred lineaments. Doctor Tsarka stayed him with a gesture.

"Be patient, Asoya Horubu. Your instincts run to violence. This," he indicated the bent figure of the artist peremptorily, "this boy has been in a desperate enterprise. He needs sympathy."

The ex-soldier resumed his seat muttering a Bushido curse on all effeminate natures. Tsarka walked the length of the study halting at the window where the river lights glowed through the mists. A tug hooted her way up stream toward a huddle of barges lying in the black shelter of the bridge span.

The artist's voice reached him in broken sobs; a voice full of the child anguish that goes with the little people of Nippon.

"I had fulfilled my task, and had left the atelier in the hands of our victims. Everything had gone with snap; there were no hitches. The American man had been converted into a blue-whiskered fool by the ray-molecule distributor; the German Baron had become aware of his spots, and was screaming for swimming baths.   Everything looked well. Even the Duchess of Marister succumbed to my invitation to view the 'Haunted Pagoda' through the radium-poisoned stereoscope.

"I gained my car outside," Inouyiti continued, "and had almost reached this house before I learned that Miss Cranstone, the lady who is my life, the flower of my soul, had entered the atelier uninvited.   The devil guided her footsteps to the hell of torture I had prepared for others.   I learned the news from an evening paper.   It is more than I can bear.   I cannot live to see her suffer!"

Doctor Tsarka eyed him coldly, his dark face kindling strangely.

"Your private love affairs are nothing to us, Inouyiti.   If this English actress has shared the radium sponge with the others, so be it. Do not harry our good comrade Horubu with your weeping."

Inouyiti rose gaping incredulously, his fingers stiffened at his side.

"I shall go from here.   The heaven that receives us after death has been shut to me!"

he almost shouted. "I shall cry for her in the dark, for ever and ever. We shall pass and repass each other throughout eternity without seeing or speaking!"

He sank back in his chair as though a hand had pushed him.

"The artistic temperament!" Horubu growled. "The stuff that destroys armies and national organizations. Tashan!"

"It is a kind of spiritual radium — a disease which suffers from eternal volition." Doctor Tsarka spoke in a sneering undertone intended for the artist's sensitive hearing.

Silence fell upon the study while Inouyiti rocked to and fro in his torment. Tsarka's head was bowed toward the lamp, his eyes devouring the evening paper which had fallen from the young artist's hand. He sighed as he read the brief, eye-searing headlines which revealed, at a glance, the story of Inouyiti's crime. He handed the paper to the silent Horubu in the corner.

"We shall gather enough fees from this holocaust to extend our operations to America," he said dreamfully. "America is the place where the million-dollar men encourage science, Horubu."

Horubu read the paper, grunting from time to time as the magnitude of the crime revealed itself.   Then, with a shrug, tossed the paper aside.

"You have planned this *coup* to catch patients for your Radium Institute, my dear Tsarka.   It may fail yet," he vouchsafed sullenly.   "I do not like these inspired propositions."

"How can we fail?"   Doctor Tsarka eyed him in good-tempered amazement.   "We set the fashion by curing Gifford Renwick.   The renowned English specialist, Sir Floyd Garston, admits that the Messonier Institute has achieved the greatest triumph in modern ophthalmic surgery.   A score of leading European and British medical journals are filling their columns with the facts of the Renwick cure.   We are famous.   The Duchess of Marister and Prince Hohenhoff will certainly go to Beatrice Messonier.   They must then choose between blindness and our fees" — he laughed.

Horubu grinned, then took a black cigar from his pocket and wolfed the edges thoughtfully.   His huge shoulders were silhouetted in an elephantine curve against the window

pane.   Puffing heavily at the cigar, his quick-
shifting eyes wandered to the figure of the
artist crouching in the chair.

"It is all like the dream of a weary nerve
specialist," he said broodingly.   "We must
take care and not push our guns too far.
Now," he paused while the cigar smoke
marbled the air above him, "it is time
we collected our loose radium and sent
it to the Messonier woman.   She will need
it."

"Inouyiti has the radium, the six grains
we took from Moritz's laboratory.   I gave
it to him in a bulb for his use at the studio.
He could not charge nor infiltrate his rays
and sponges without it."

Doctor Tsarka turned to the sobbing boy
artist and touched his bent shoulder.

"Where is the radium bulb?" he asked.
"It is much safer in my keeping, Inouyiti.
Beatrice Messonier may require it for cura-
tive purposes immediately."

The young artist shrank from his touch,
the dark, unfathomable eyes peering into
his own.

"I took it from the bulb and —" his voice
trembled to the snapping point — "and put

it in the rubber finger I wear.   The idea came from you, Teroni."

"Where is the finger?" Tsarka's hand stiffened like a garroter's on his shoulder. "Where is it?"

Inouyiti quailed under the merciless eyes; his breath came in sharp expulsions.

"I left it in the studio," he said faintly. "I forgot it in the rush to get away.   Three hours ago I sent the woman to search the atelier.   I have not heard from her since."

"Left it in the studio!" Doctor Tsarka repeated the words with scarce a lift in his voice.   "Six thousand pounds worth of radium!"

He stared bleakly at the cowering form in the chair, a dry grin of hate on his lips.

Horubu leaned spellbound from the shadows, his great neck and shoulders swaying slightly.

"You pulseless dog; what have you done!"

"Silence!"   There was a tremor of passion in Doctor Tsarka's voice.   The years of toil and privations through which he had passed seemed to flash in his great eyes.   Defeat, colossal and profound, was leaping to meet him, and after the sullen years of labour and travail.   All gone in the turn of a fool's brain.   He glanced at the cowering Inouyiti as though he would strike.

"Your mind was too full of your own safety to remember our priceless stock of radium. Six thousand pounds worth!"

"The radium was our life's blood," Horubu snarled.   "Our fighting breath.   It was our white weapon.   Tashan!"

Inouyiti staggered from his seat, revolt, mutiny in his eyes.   "Take care, Teroni Tsarka, and you, Horubu, the wolf!   The task allotted was too heavy for me.   I had to control six people."

"Six paint-mad fools!" Horubu retorted.

Inouyiti's wrath threatened to hurl him at his bull-throated tormentor.   "The woman McGuire will have found the radium.   I shall hear from her this evening," he cried.

"There is a telephone where she lives." Doctor Tsarka took a card from his pocket. "The number is written here.   Go you, Horubu, to the bureau — there is one a couple of streets away — and ascertain whether this Rose McGuire picked up the rubber finger."

Horubu took the card with the telephone number, and departed noiselessly.   The little

Japanese doctor turned to the trembling boy artist the moment the street door closed.

"Because I believed that our stock of pure radium was better kept in a single bulb I entrusted it to you. It was a foolish experiment. Our chance in life now depends on whether this woman McGuire was quick enough to carry out your orders."

"If it is lost?"

"We are beggars — worse. Beatrice Messonier cannot cope with the sudden rush of aristocratic patients unless she has fresh supplies of pure radium. You do not understand her intricate, light-developing processes. Her instruments need to be constantly filamented. She must have radium."

"We can obtain more. My pictures are worth a thousand pounds," pleaded the despairing artist.

"A thousand Gehennas!" Tsarka's fingers snapped in his face. "Who will buy your pictures now after the studio affair? And if we had money," he continued sharply, "we could not obtain immediate supplies. The European laboratories are under police surveillance. The factory at Bermondsey would not sell us a grain. You have created a devil's corner for us, Inouyiti!"

In the silence that followed his bitter tirade Horubu's footsteps were heard in the passage. He entered with tigerish suddenness, his fierce eyes seeking Inouyiti.

"The McGuire is being shadowed!" His voice sounded like an impact of steel. His squat figure halted in the doorway. "The dog Renwick was in the studio when she arrived. He made her confess everything!"

"The radium?" Tsarka's frail body trembled like an overwrought instrument. He crouched aside as one about to receive a blow.

Horubu sat down, his clenched fists resting on his knees. "Renwick is carrying it in his pocket. This artistic temperament of Inouyiti's has severed our arteries, as General Oyama once said. Give me a cigar."

Doctor Tsarka pushed a small box across the table, while the ex-soldier rifled its cont' ts for the strongest weed.

I did not consent to this fool device of concealing six thousand pounds' worth of radium in a stupid rubber finger. Why was

I not consulted?" he demanded, the cigar flattened between his teeth.

"You were not here," Tsarka answered. "The finger appealed to me as an excellent device for carrying the radium. Glass bulbs break easily. Inouyiti always wore the finger in public. It did not seem probable that he would leave a finger behind, eh, Horubu?"

"A childish experiment!" growled the ex-soldier. "Its failure costs us blood and brains. Hi yah!" He yawned with tiger-ish gusto, as though resigned to the misfortune which the young artist had brought about.

Doctor Tsarka paled slightly as he turned again to Inouyiti. "You must seek out Gifford Renwick," he said, with an effort. "He may not discover the radium for weeks. He is almost sure to put the rubber finger in his pocket and, like most Englishmen, forget its existence."

"What shall I say to Renwick?" Inouyiti asked faintly. "I am known to him."

Tsarka shrugged wearily. "Shoot him on the pavement. It is our only chance. Horubu will be at hand with a fast car to snatch the rubber finger from his pocket."

"He may have already delivered it to his employer." Horubu spoke from the corner, his sullen brow creased in thought.

"There is always the good chance that the radium may have escaped his notice," Doctor Tsarka urged. "He may carry it about as a clue for weeks. Who knows! Surely the attempt is worth making."

Horubu moved in his chair like an animal disturbed. His sullen features relaxed by degrees as though his *confrère's* scheme had seized his imagination.

"Tshu!" A slight hissing noise escaped him as the pungent cigar smoke oozed from his mouth. "Inouyiti shall go. He will be caught and hanged for certain. But hanging is better for Inouyiti than *hari kari*. There will be no more exhibitions of 'Haunted Pagodas.' The public shall have a rest."

The young artist crouched low in the chair, staring dull-eyed at the two men while they arranged, with merciless precision, the manner of his undoing.

"I will not shoot Renwick!" he declared, unable to suppress his wild fears. "You shall not decide my fate — you two!"

Horubu's fist swung from the shadows as

though to grapple the swaying figure in the chair. Tsarka interposed.

"The boy has his beliefs, Horubu. We have ours." He placed a finger on the artist's shoulder. "There will be no more cures at the Institute. The English lady who has turned your soul to fire, the Miss Cranstone whose eyes have retained your radium poison, shall be left to the mercy of the English medical prigs. Beatrice Messonier would have cured her as she cured Renwick. To-morrow I close the Institute and," he laughed sharply, "there will be three blind mice waiting on the steps — calling for mercy and the light they will never again behold!"

Inouyiti flinched as though naked steel had touched him. "You will not commit this last infamy, Teroni Tsarka. Let me expiate . . . A son of the *Samurai* knows how to suffer and obey. Your wishes are mine. I am ready."

He spoke quietly now, his head bent in silent submission, his thin, shapely hands thrust out into the lamp glow.

Doctor Tsarka sighed, and then glanced meaningly at the bull-necked ex-soldier.

"Are you also ready?" he asked simply.

Horubu waved his fuming cigar-butt, and was instantly seized by a fit of coughing that almost bent him to the floor. Recovering slowly, he thrust his asthma-congested face nearer the light.

"Give me a good car, Teroni. Let Inouyiti do the shooting. I will be near to strip Renwick if necessary. The rubber finger may be in his pocket. Then" — he paused as the coughing fit threatened to strangle him — "then, if there is a crowd of police and other fools to obstruct me I will give them a little exhibition of Indian Juggernaut work. I must have a good car, though," he added, wiping his purple face. "One that will smash up a crowd like Oyama's nine-inch shells. Ayati! I am ready, Teroni."

CHAPTER X

DOCTOR TSARKA was never a victim of his own impulses. In ordering Soto Inouyiti to shoot Gifford Renwick he had done so believing that his existence depended upon the swift recovery of the radium concealed within the joints of the little rubber finger.

Horubu rose from his corner near the window, his animal eyes searching the study from corner to corner.

"I want a pair of motor-goggles and a chin-mask. That red tie of Inouyiti's will hang us all unless it is burnt," he growled with a nod in the artist's direction.

The desired articles were brought in by a quick-footed coolie servant, while Doctor Tsarka permitted himself a sharp examination of Inouyiti's wearing apparel.

"You must dress for the adventure," he said gently. "An American army hat and a suggestion of a beard will give you a Bohemian appearance. You keep

such things for the use of your models, do
you not?"

The boy shivered as the gleam of Horubu's
revolver lit the dark folds of his driving coat.
"I will do what you wish," he muttered fear-
fully. "Only I must have your promise that
Miss Cranstone shall be treated by Beatrice
Messonier."

Doctor Tsarka regarded him sombrely.
"Bring back the rubber finger, Inouyiti.
Miss Cranstone shall be cured. Now go to
your room. Fix yourself for a meeting with
Renwick, and shoot straight."

Horubu waddled impatiently about the
study while the young artist retired to complete his facial disguise. He paused at intervals in his limping promenade to inspect,
by the lamp glow, his cartridge-filled revolver.

"I want your chauffeur's license, Teroni,"
he said huskily. "There is a German, near
Victoria, who has the car I want. It has a
torpedo body, a snout of steel. It was built
in Paris for a Russian army surgeon who did
ambulance work in Manchuria. It is an
ugly machine, and was brought to London
by a builder who used it for a model. The

German at the garage wants me to buy it. He is willing to allow me a few trial runs."

"You are going to paint the wheels," Tsarka questioned unmoved, "with English blood?"

"If the English fools get in my way to-night there will be a red car in the garage to-morrow," Horubu grunted.

Inouyiti returned, an American army hat drawn over his brow. The change in his appearance elicited a mutter of admiration from both men. He was no longer the sloping-shouldered boy artist of eighteen. A few pencil strokes had given length to his round Japanese features. A wisp of beard, torpedo pointed, completed the change. Horubu clapped his shoulder with affected bonhomie.

"Dressed for killing, eh, my pretty Inouyiti! This night your name shall ring through London. Your photographs will be in all the shop windows."

Now that the young artist's rôle, in the prospective shooting expedition, had been decided, Horubu affected a grim pleasantry that was not devoid of affection, for Inouyiti and the ex-soldier had enjoyed a certain camaraderie together in London.

To Inouyiti the shooting of Gifford Renwick meant certain arrest, and death eventually, in expiation of his crime. The thought
scarcely caused him an instant's regret. It
was the memory of the studio tragedy that
bludgeoned his conscience now, of Violet
Cranstone, the one woman who had stirred
his Asiatic soul to love and tenderness. He
had never hoped to gain her affection — she
was too far removed, socially, racially. All
the fires of his transparent genius could not
win her back to him.

Doctor Tsarka took his hand, as he joined
Horubu in the hall, and permitted an emo-
tional tremor to soften the blade-edge of his
words.

"Adieu, Inouyiti; we shall remember you as
a brave boy.   If you fail to-night there is no
hope for us. Shoot low; grip him when he
falls and get to his pockets. Throw the
rubber finger to Horubu. Now go!"

The young artist muttered an inaudible
good-by, then stepped into the street, chin
in the air, his eyes aflame. The fragments of
a *Samurai* war song broke from him only to
be checked by his sullen-browed companion.

"We must reach Victoria, boy. A train

leaves here at eight o'clock. This Renwick often reports the day's work to his chief between nine and ten. If he is later we shall meet the theatre crowds."

Inouyiti meekly hummed his Japanese song as they tramped to the station. The end had come and he was no longer afraid. All his life he had struggled to attain eminence at his craft. Success had almost crowned his efforts until his meeting with Doctor Tsarka. The little nerve specialist had advanced him large sums of money to assist him in his fight for fame, but each fresh loan only plunged him deeper into debt. His pictures did not sell rapidly, and since his appearance in London he had acquired expensive tastes. The simple habits of his early life no longer sufficed. French dinners, theatre parties, and the society of English ladies had taken their place. He was no longer the homely boy artist who had journeyed from Tokyo, with his brushes and canvas, to conquer the artistic soul of Great Britain. The fire of genius was still in his pulse; colour and vision still sobbed for expression. Yet here was the end of life — a gallows in an English gaol!

In a few sane moments that flashed upon

him, at intervals, his mind went back to the
scene in the studio, the men and women he
had blinded and maimed at the bidding of
Teroni Tsarka. What madness had led him
into the compact! Tsarka had assured him
that it was all a joke that would make the
English laugh. They would laugh, Tsarka
had assured him, at the Baron with the spots,
at the American millionaire with the purple
whiskers. But Teroni Tsarka had said nothing about the horrible effects of the radium
sponge concealed within the specially arranged stereoscope. Neither had the Fates
warned him that Violet Cranstone would walk
into the midst of his devilish manipula-
tions.

Horubu sat beside him in the train until
Victoria was reached. Here the gruff ex-
soldier hurried him down a maze of streets
where the traffic enveloped them like a mill-
race. Horubu halted at the door of a garage
kept by an oily-tongued German, and briefly
made known his wants. The German shook
hands cordially with Horubu in the badly lit
passage, where half a dozen dilapidated cars
filled the background.

The ex-soldier's glance wandered over the

scrap-heap of derelict automobiles, a look of feigned disappointment in his eyes.

"The old French machine not here," he said in his incomplete English, his squat bulk half hid in the shadow of the gate. "I want it to look at."

The German smiled reassuringly. "I keep id in der back garage because id distracts my customers. Dey say id is such a big car."

Horubu affected an air of sullen surprise. "The machine is heavy," he admitted; "too heavy for scout work." He fumbled with some papers in his pocket as though in search of a letter.

"A friend of mine is going to the Congo next month. He wants a big, ugly car for the bad roads, a car that will not to pieces go when it strikes a tree stump."

The German evinced a business-like interest in the ex-soldier's statement. "De old tumbril haf a record for heavy work," he laughed. "Id vas an old Russian army machine, und vas vort a hundred and fifty pounds as a model. Coom into der shed und haf a look."

Horubu followed him, leaving Inouyiti standing in the shadow of the gate. The German opened the shed door and lit a lamp

suspended from an overhead beam. In the
centre of the garage stood a low torpedo-
shaped car, conspicuous for its heavy mount-
ings and axles. The proprietor patted its
steel-belted face as though it were a man-
killing tiger.

"Id belong to an army surgeon, und passed
into der hands ob Lieutenant Scolitz of der
Second Army Corps." The German spoke in a
confidential tone to Horubu, stooping over the
copper-framed wind-screen.

"Id vas at Mukden where der fightin' vas
und id did some rear-guard work," he concluded with a deep chuckle.

"Tashan! I remember," nodded the ex-
soldier, passing his black hand over the clutch
and gear-boxes. "Scolitz was cut off by a
detachment of the Twenty-third Infantry."

The German gaped a little at the announcement, then, detecting something of the soldier
in Horubu, laughed good-humouredly. "Dot
accounts for dese scratches, eh?'

He indicated a network of scars that ran
diagonally across the steel-snouted machine.
"Scolitz drove der car over der bayonets,"
he added with a hoarse laugh. "He milled
his way troo der Twenty-third, eh, mein

friendt, und joined Kuropatkin like a good soldier."

"Tsh!" Horubu strode round the machine, a critical scowl on his brow.

"It's a big scrap-heap, but if it has — pace ——"

"Id leaps — ieaps!" the German exclaimed. "Id can run down an express midout shifting a screw."

"Get it ready!" Horubu commanded. "I will return it before morning after my friend has looked at it well."

Twenty minutes later the "torpedo" car glided from the garage with Inouyiti seated low in the submarine-shaped "poop." The car, under the ex-soldier's hand, moved with a peculiar sobbing noise in the direction of the International Inquiry Bureau. The young artist had drawn his hat over his eyes and his thoughts ran again to the scene in the studio where he pictured, with flowing imagery, the tragic moment when Violet Cranstone rushed unbidden to the deadly stereoscope.

Horubu spoke once as the car swung into Whitehall, and his voice sounded above the vibrating throb of the cylinders.

"You are a good shot, Inouyiti?" he asked.

"Yes." The artist answered with his head down. He was thinking of a blind face and a pair of radium-scarred eyes.

Horubu grunted, his chin near the window-screen. "Don't mistake your man. Put out your hand and take this pistol."

He thrust the heavy service revolver into the slim, tight-clenched hand, and again his glance returned to the wind-screen.

"You know Renwick well, eh?"

"Quite. He is taller than most English or Americans. He has a good face and womanish eyes." Inouyiti spoke in a scarce audible voice, his head almost between his knees. "I shall not mistake him."

"Men with womanish eyes have a knack of facing the fire," Horubu grumbled. "Take care and watch him."

The car drew up with a sliding gurr about twenty yards from the entrance to the International Inquiry Bureau.

"When I light a cigarette — fire," Horubu whispered. "Keep your weapon ready; he may be here at any moment."

CHAPTER XI

GIFFORD RENWICK was vastly interested in the fluorescent rays which grew more brilliant as he sheltered the rubber finger from the electric glow. The carpeted floor, beneath the table, was illumined by a flood of amethyst light that spread to his hand and clothes with the suddenness of a Röntgen-ray.

Gifford was not eager to replace the rubber finger in his pocket. A sudden fear of its radio-active properties came upon him. Wrapping it in his 'kerchief gingerly he left the restaurant and succeeded in obtaining a small empty chocolate box from an adjoining confectioner's. Dropping the rubber digit in the soft paper at the bottom he was able to examine with more safety the cause of the light-emissions.

Only one known element **was** capable of such tremendous molecular activity. And he divined in a flash that Inouyiti's false finger contained a large quantity of pure

radium. Further reflection induced the belief that the six grains of radium which had
been stolen from the laboratory of Professor
Moritz lay concealed in the hollow of the
rubber finger!

With all his cunning and duplicity Doctor
Tsarka had failed to hold the precious substance which had cost him many months of
labour and toil to acquire. A thrill of pleasure
seized Gifford as he strode in the direction
of the International Inquiry Bureau, the
small cardboard box gripped firmly in his
hand. To have recovered the six thousand
pounds' worth of radium seemed like one of
Fate's compensations after his bitter experiences in the past.

Whitehall and its immediate precincts were
in a state of unusual quietude as he hurried
toward the Bureau. At Horseguards Avenue
he paused irresolutely as though some long
dead instinct had been startled to life, goading
him into a state of unusual alertness. Some
distance ahead, wrapped in the night fog,
panted a long-bodied, steel-hipped automobile.

Gifford's eye traversed the broad column
of shadow which slanted from the windows

of the adjacent buildings, and, in that brief
glance, he detected the figure of Soto Inouyiti
standing near the portico.

There was nothing in the artist's pose to
attract attention; it was the grotesque outline
of the automobile that quickened his curiosity;
its huge tumbril-like body, the great steel
snout that seemed capable of boring through
an army.   But, most of all, Gifford's instincts
swung him wide of the bull-necked figure
squatting behind the clutch.

Within fifteen feet of Inouyiti he halted
sharply because the young artist had become
aware of his approach.   Incidentally the man
in the car lit a cigarette.

Gifford checked an exclamation as his eyes
followed the up-slanting pistol in the artist's
fist.   A moment later he saw the white flash,
felt the heart-shaking report as the bullet
sobbed past his face.

"The deuce take you!   What are you firing
at?"

Gifford remained stationary for a fraction
of time, then a forward leap took him within
three feet of his assailant.   Inouyiti's hand
deviated slightly from the line of fire, and the
accompanying flash lit up his eyes.   Gifford

" ' DRAG THE BEAST OUT ! TIE HIM TO THE CAR WITH
HIS OWN ROPE ! ' STICKS AND UMBRELLAS SMOTE AND
STABBED IN HORUBU'S DIRECTION "

ducked nimbly, his right hand smashing upward at the levelled arm.

Inouyiti screamed a word in the vernacular
as the smoking weapon was twisted from his
grasp. With a cleverly executed armlock
Gifford brought him to the half-turn before
the artist had regained his equilibrium.

Gifford breathed sharply, his eyes questing
over the charcoal-lined features, the tag of
false beard which had fallen, in the struggle,
to the pavement.

"You must come with me, Soto. There's
a warrant out for your arrest in connection
with that studio business. Don't struggle or
your wrists may get broken."

A small crowd had been attracted by the
revolver shots. Gifford waved back a dozen
hands that sought to render assistance.
Inouyiti hung limply in his grasp, his frail
figure palpitating with exhaustion after his
desperate scuffle. Slowly the young Englishman urged him forward in the direction of
Scotland Yard, hoping to obtain police help
before the crowd increased.

Passing the low-bodied automobile with his
assailant, the young detective observed a
sudden movement on the driver's part. In-

stantly Gifford sought to evade a noosed coil
of rope that circled with unerring judgment
above his head. Swiftly the loop descended,
and was drawn with a savage jerk about his
shoulders and arms. Simultaneously he felt
himself jerked from his feet toward the front
wheels of the throbbing car.

Horubu, with unparalleled audacity, moved
the car forward a couple of yards and then,
reaching out, made fast the rope to the heavy
iron step under the door.

Gifford struggled desperately to slip his
arms from the octopus-like noose, his fingers
striving to grasp Inouyiti's revolver, which
had fallen within reach.

Without haste or trepidation, Horubu
slipped from his seat and caught up the semi-
conscious artist from the pavement and
dropped him, without ceremony, into the car.
With a panther-like movement he was back
in his place, his great hands encircling the
clutch.

The crowd appeared to divine his intentions,
for as the car slid forward a friendly knife
slashed the rope which threatened to drag
Gifford through the streets of Westminster.

Horubu snapped a warning oath at the

crowd of arms and shoulders that sought to bar his progress. A woman screamed at him from the pavement, for she had noted the grim race-hatred that flamed in his eyes. A stone whipped past her, smashing the wind-screen almost in his face.

"Drag the beast out!"

"Tie him to the car with his own rope!"

Sticks and umbrellas smote and stabbed in Horubu's direction. For an instant it seemed as though the clutch would not answer. The car sobbed and fretted near the pavement like an animal held in check.

The hand of a night watchman closed on Horubu's neck as he stooped over a refractory lever. Another grabbed the supine Inouyiti lying at his feet.

"They're Japs. . . . By Jove! Have 'em out. Turn the iron trap on top of 'em!"

The Japanese ex-soldier shook off the watchman's grip, and his eye measured the throng which threatened to cut off his retreat. Another moment and he would be out of the car under the feet of the excited Londoners.

The refractory lever responded to his touch, and the whale-backed machine rushed forward into the tight-packed zone of arms and faces.

A man, leaning across the front-wheel guard, was flung stammering to the curb as though a bison had pitched him clear of the track. Gifford had gained his feet, in a half-dazed condition, his arms tingling and swollen where the noose had gripped.

With some discretion the crowd scattered in front of the steel-hipped auto, allowing it to swing by. At the street corner, where the traffic grew denser as the theatre cabs swept past, another crowd, attracted by the screams and shouting voices, appeared at the street entrance.

The auto moaned hoarsely, like a bull about to charge. Half a dozen enraged citizens clung to the wheel-guards and sides in their efforts to drag the Japanese ex-soldier from his seat.

A sudden throw in of the clutch swayed the heavy-bodied car on the sidewalk; another, executed with the dexterity of an experienced chauffeur, sent her at full speed in a line with the wall. The men clinging to the wheel-guards were brushed off like flies.

Horubu grinned as the released auto dashed from the sidewalk into the midst of the bewildered crowd. As a knife slides through bread so it separated and mowed down the flying pedestrians. Right and left it charged, grinding, slamming beneath its wheels the men and women who sought to reach a place of safety.

Horubu hurtled through Whitehall into Northumberland Avenue, slackening speed near the embankment only when the shouts of the outraged citizens had died away.

"We must separate," he said to the slowly recovering young artist. "Get up, pull your silly wits together."

Halting the machine in the shadow of the railway arch, he alighted and hauled Inouyiti unceremoniously into the road. Then, with a glance over his shoulder at the car, hurried the boy artist toward Waterloo Bridge.

"There will be a hue and cry," he said hoarsely. "We must get to shelter."

"But . . . we have accomplished nothing!" Inouyiti almost sobbed. "After the killing and the mutilations . . ."

"We have the radium *cache*." Horubu tapped his huge pocket significantly. "The dog, Renwick, was carrying our fortunes in a chocolate box. Only for my American lariat he would have carried you to the gallows. Assoba! We part here. Go back to Tsarka."

Horubu touched his shoulder lightly and then walked sharply in the direction of the bridge lamps.

CHAPTER XII

AN OVERWHELMING sense of defeat seized Gifford Renwick when he discovered that Horubu had forced his "torpedo" car through the crowd, leaving in his wheel-tracks a score of maimed and crippled pedestrians.

He was conscious of Tony Hackett's voice addressing him above the babel of the crowd.

".Come away, Gif; the ambulance people are attending the wounded. Great Scott, those Japanese radium sneaks are fighting us within a stone's throw of Scotland Yard."

Half a dozen emergency police-cars had left Whitehall in the hope of catching up with the torpedo-shaped machine and its two occupants. Gifford was not likely to forget the bull-necked figure of Horubu, even the chin-mask and goggles had not concealed from him the personality of Doctor Tsarka's fighting lieutenant.

"The little nerve doctor has got us

whipped," Tony declared as they pressed in the direction of the International Inquiry Bureau. "Just now the City is crowded with Japanese visitors who have come here to see the Exhibition at Shepherd's Bush. If we arrest the wrong lot of Japs there'll be trouble. The Government would start calling us names."

Gifford made an unbiased statement of the affair to his chief, while the news of Inouyiti's second outrage roared through the City. Scores of police-cars traversed the metropolitan area in the hope of encountering the big Manchurian automobile.

"If we assume that Doctor Tsarka and his people intend remaining in London, we have the task of separating them from six or seven million people," Anthony Coleman averred.

"In spite of the Exhibition there are not more than a thousand Japs in the county of Middlesex." Tony Hackett had entered the room with Gifford. His advice in the present instance was considered invaluable.

"Scotland Yard could round up the lot in twenty-four hours if it wanted. Of course, there's the diplomatic aspect, international ruptures and all that kind of music if violent hands were laid on the wrong people."

"You can't round up criminals who live in underground laboratories," Gifford declared vehemently. "Tsarka is a human mole; he's never seen by the tradespeople. He owns a private car and changes his number about."

"I've been trying to pick up his car numbers without giving away the show to the metropolitan police," Hackett confided.

"Want the credit yourself, eh?" his chief asked.

"For Coleman's International Inquiry Bureau," Tony laughed. "I'm not supplying Scotland Yard with gratuitous information."

Gifford returned, the following day, to the house of Mrs. Cranstone, in the hope that Inouyiti might be driven to pay a final visit to the young comedy actress, who still endured the torments of radium blindness.

Mrs. Cranstone's face showed signs of some recent emotion as she greeted the young detective. Her voice quivered strangely. It was evident that some unfavourable development in her daughter's condition had occurred since the previous evening.

"You must see Madame Messonier," he advised, a thought surging through his mind that Miss Cranstone had succumbed to the terrors of the long night.

Mrs. Cranstone was scarce able to repress her grief as she led him into the drawing room. "We lost no time in visiting the Messonier Institute," she began in dejected tones. "I could not endure Violet's agony an instant longer. After Sir Floyd left here the colour storms became frightful. I put her into a cab and drove to the Institute."

"You saw madame?"

"No; the servant assured us that madame could not see us until this morning. So Violet passed a night of torment without medical assistance of any kind."

Mrs. Cranstone sobbed a little at the memory of her daughter's sufferings.

"This morning at eight o'clock," she continued, "we again called at the Radium Institute. Madame Messonier very graciously consented to examine my daughter. Her diagnosis, I must admit, was very skilfully conducted. She assured me that radium poisoning was the cause of Violet's partial blindness. There was absolutely no cause for alarm if proper remedies were applied without delay."

Gifford nodded approvingly. "You may trust her," he declared with enthusiasm. "For am I not a living witness to her infallible skill!"

Mrs. Cranstone inclined her head somewhat doubtfully. "I might agree with you, Mr. Renwick, if it were not for her fee. The amount she asked is simply absurd."

"I paid her two hundred guineas," he admitted. "One does not hesitate when a certain person drives."

"Two hundred guineas!" Mrs. Cranstone cried out her words. "Madame Messonier refused to begin her treatment unless a fee of two thousand guineas were paid in advance. It is monstrous, Mr. Renwick!"

Gifford winced. The sum appeared to him incredible. He could not believe that Beatrice Messonier would seek to wring so ruinous a fee from a suffering patient. He turned to Mrs. Cranstone, a touch of regret in his voice.

"There is no other radium specialist in England. I begin to fear that other powers than Beatrice Messonier are directing the fortunes of the Institute. The shareholders probably," he added, half to himself.

It had not occurred to him that Beatrice Messonier might have become the mere servant of a dividend-hunting gang of shareholders who had taken advantage of her unique powers to force wealthy patients into the paying of abnormal fees. The idea set him wondering whether the Radium Institute had any real connection with Tsarka. At first the thought appeared monstrous, unjust, until the sheer weight of facts balanced him into a sudden belief of Madame Messonier's complicity. Unthinkable as it was to him he could not disassociate the recent Tsarka-Inouyiti outrages from the Messonier Institute. Yet how came it that Pepio had risked her liberty to supply him with funds to meet the Institute fees, he asked himself?

With some difficulty he calmed the whirlwind of thoughts, generated by his hasty inductions, and turned again to the sobbing woman beside him. He knew that Violet Cranstone's sufferings would end only when the devils of radium had completely extinguished her sight.

"You must make one more appeal to Madame," he urged. "Delay will certainly mean a living death for your daughter even though you send her to the Paris Institute. A few more hours and the light will be gone forever. Try again!"

He spoke in tones of genuine passion that reached the half-blind girl in the adjoining apartment.

Strangely enough his appeal merely evoked a wave of matronly wrath from the hard-pressed Mrs. Cranstone.

"This Madame Messonier is — is impossible even to the well-to-do. I begged her to operate on my daughter, begged on my knees. I explained how difficult it was to raise so large a sum. And . . . she froze me with those terrible eyes. You know how they burn!" she cried disjointedly. "I will not beg again. I will try the Paris Institute; it may not be too late!'

Gifford could easily understand Mrs. Cranstone's outburst. Without influence or friends her whole life had been dedicated to her daughter's well-being. There had been pecuniary hardships and heroic self-sacrifices to enable Violet to maintain her position on the stage. And now, by a stroke from a mad artist's brain, she was threatened with complete loss of sight.

"Two thousand guineas is more than I can command unless our few worldly securities are handed over to this professional vampire," Mrs. Cranstone declared with rising wrath.

Gifford readily forgave her anger when he thought of the blind girl actress. Yet he was loath to think of the angel-like Beatrice Messonier as a merciless charlatan. Some unknown influence was forcing her into demanding colossal fees.

In the silence that followed Mrs. Cranstone's outburst, Gifford's alert brain was shaping a fresh attack on the gang of Japanese adventurers. His plans streamed molten through his mind as he unconsciously paced the room.

Mrs. Cranstone's scarce audible sobbing aroused him from his swift thoughts. If Violet's sight was to be saved the question of fees must not stand in the way. Assuming that Beatrice was implacable, then the mother must yield. Each moment wasted only increased the nerve-destroying elements at work on the young girl's eyes.

With an impressive gesture Mrs. Cranstone drew him into the adjoining room, where sat the unhappy young actress, her hands drawn tightly over her radium-tortured retina.

Gifford's nature was too boyish and tender not to feel something of pain and regret at her tragic misadventure.

"I am — I am so sorry, Miss Cranstone," was all he could say. "We must be very patient and we will win through."

She raised her head at the sound of his voice; her lips grew less tight. She seemed to be holding herself from the barbed shafts of light that pierced her throbbing eyelids.

"Thank you for your good wishes, Mr. Renwick," she half whispered. "At present my head feels as if it were passing through a cyclone of flying stars. Is — is that how you felt?"

"Hot irons and comets' tails," he replied, in his attempt to cheer her. "You are through the worst now. In a week you will be laughing at your experiences among the little radium imps."

Gifford could not rid himself of the idea of his responsibility in her tragic misadventure. He blamed himself for permitting Doctor Tsarka to escape him. A genius of the profession, he told himself, would have smashed the gang of radium terrors at the outset.

With a final word of consolation to the young actress he followed Mrs. Cranstone to the door.

"I am going to interview Madame Messonier." Gifford controlled himself slightly. "Will you bring Miss Cranstone to the Institute at twelve o'clock?"

"It is ten now. I cannot raise two thousand guineas in two hours."

"There will be no need," Gifford said quietly. "All I ask is that you bring your daughter to the Institute."

"But you cannot influence that woman!" Mrs. Cranstone spoke with a sobbing emphasis that sharpened the young detective's resolution. "You cannot compel her to effect a cure if she is unwilling."

"Be there at twelve." Gifford paused in the hall, his hand outstretched. "I give you my word that Beatrice Messonier shall begin Miss Cranstone's cure at once."

CHAPTER XIII

IN THE street Gifford encountered Norry
Blake, a young reporter, who hailed him
with the camaraderie of a Fleet Street
Bohemian. Blake was abrim with news of
the recent studio tragedy.

"See here, Gif," he began, with profes-
sional alertness, "I've just interviewed Prince
Hohenhoff's people, and they say that His
Highness is hopelessly blind."

Gifford shrugged in a non-committal way.
"There are physicians capable of treating
radium poisoning," he affirmed. "What
about the Messonier Institute?"

Blake shook his head despondently. "The
Duchess of Marister has been there, but has
scarcely recovered the shock. It was worse
than the studio calamity. Messonier's fees
are the talk of the city."

"How much for the Duchess?"

"Five thousand guineas down or no con-
sultations. The Messonier's reputation is
rising in fashionable circles. People are

asking who she is. There's nothing like a Himalayan fee to elevate one in the public estimation," Blake affirmed.

"And the Spotted Baron?" Gifford inquired humbly. "Is he at large?"

"He's gone to the Messonier," the journalist laughed. "For the modest sum of three thousand guineas she has promised to eradicate his spots by a new process of radio-magnetism."

"And the American millionaire?"

"The Messonier didn't get him. He left here for Paris last night. Reckons he can get the purple out of his hair and whiskers for half the money in France. Cute fellows these Americans," Blake vouchsafed. "They'd go to the North Pole to save their hair. Have a drink, Renwick?"

"Thanks, no; I've just recovered from an attack of radium poisoning," Gifford retorted innocently. "Good-by!"

Proceeding hastily in the direction of Huntingdon Street, Gifford's spirits sank to zero at the thought of meeting the incomparable Beatrice Messonier. He could not think of her as a heartless practitioner bent on extracting the last guinea from her de-

spairing patients. He was aware that many
West End specialists charged unheard-of
fees when the occasion warranted, but he
could not bring to mind the name of an
English physician who closed his operating
rooms to the sick and desperate.

Gifford was not particularly distressed because a few German art patrons had been subjected to a more or less farcical indignity. The
wealthy Duchess of Marister could take care
of herself. It was the spectacle of the partially blinded young comedy actress which
caused his humanity to cry within him. The
two thousand guineas demanded by Beatrice
Messonier would ruin Mrs. Cranstone and
her daughter. While every eye was turned
upon the sufferings of a pride-wounded
German baron and princeling, no one had
come forward to offer the slightest sympathy or advice to the friendless mother and
daughter.

In his innocent, boyish way Gifford had
sincerely admired the madonna-faced daughter of the Japanese nerve specialist. At
another time he had fancied himself attracted toward the brilliant-eyed Beatrice
Messonier, the woman whose skill had lifted

him from darkness and despair. Both these women had exhibited mercy and tenderness toward him at a time when madness threatened to release him from his torment. Yet — he strove to crush the thought, as one crushes a weed of poisonous growth — his clear brain already perceived the links in the chain of an infamous conspiracy which bound Beatrice Messonier to Teroni Tsarka, Pepio with the fiendish boy artist, Soto Inouyiti.

Gifford had not yet suffered that hardening of mind and body which usually results from a life of incessant intercourse with the criminal classes. He could not bring himself to the point of interrogating Beatrice Messonier upon a subject which might reveal her complicity in the most dastardly outrage of the century. He could, however, investigate the business organization of the Radium Institute, could scrutinize and sift out the names of its founders and patrons, if any.

Beatrice Messonier was the one woman in England or America who had, more than any other, divined the curative properties of radium. Dr. Teroni Tsarka, on the other hand, had studied the new and wonderful element as a nerve poison, a weapon to be used against humanity to suit his own nefarious ends. By creating a "corner" in a certain curative agent, he might with skill and organization also create a special ailment among certain rich people that would necessitate instant treatment at the Messonier Institute.

The scheme would have appeared wild and improbable to any other investigator than Gifford Renwick. He had suffered the deadly radium sponge in Tsarka's laboratory, and he had lived to experience the miraculous healing powers of Beatrice Messonier.

Surely, he argued, it was not accident which had sent him to the Institute? It came upon him now like a thunderclap that the wily Jap specialist had used him as the principal advertising medium for his new-found devilries. The cheque for two hundred guineas had partially involved him, for he was now certain that Tsarka had prevailed upon his daughter to seek him out and bribe him to silence with the much-needed cash. It was this cheque which had led Gifford astray. Madame Messonier had taken it from him, and had, no doubt, returned it to

Doctor Tsarka without presenting it at the bank. It had been given him to emphasize the illusion that Tsarka was in no way connected with the Institute.

No one could prevent Beatrice Messonier demanding a colossal fee if she chose. When rich patients went to her, suffering from an apparently incurable complaint, she was at liberty to name any fee if her system of treatment proved efficacious. There were men and women in England and America who paid huge sums to medical practitioners whenever they provided a remedy for their chronic ailments.

The gang of Japanese specialists had seized upon radium, the newly discovered element, as a means to their nefarious ends. Its curative properties were in part unknown; until Beatrice Messonier had demonstrated its miraculous qualities as applied to certain forms of ophthalmic surgery. Gifford could hardly understand how Doctor Tsarka had become acquainted with this young genius of the laboratory. She may have met him at one of the various medical congresses. . . . But Gifford felt certain that it was upon her infallible skill that the little Japanese doctor had founded his Machiavellian schemes.

Once Beatrice became an acknowledged specialist in certain forms of radio-active surgery, it would only require judgment and organization to fill her consulting rooms with patients whose only hope lay in her infallible system.

When Teroni Tsarka boasted of the simple way he had extracted the six grains of radium from Moritz's laboratory he had unwittingly taught Gifford to think like a Jap. The forming of a huge medical trust was one of the schemes which had escaped British and American financiers. It had been left to a small, undersized man, named Tsarka, to invent a system whereby scores of wealthy people might be driven to pay huge fees to escape permanent blindness or other maladies which his agents might suddenly inflict upon them.

The studio outrage illustrated the methods of the Tsarka organization. Four wealthy art patrons had been lured into a carefully prepared operating chamber decked out to resemble an artist's atelier. The studio, as Gifford had discovered, was a network of

skilfully arranged magnesium wires and insulators. The little coterie of art connoisseurs had been persuaded to examine a certain
picture through a radium-poisoned stereoscope. The effect of this little operation
was to place half a dozen radium-poisoned
victims on the medical market. There followed, naturally, a desire on the part of the
victims to consult a specialist of undoubted
ability. Where was such a specialist to be
found in London? One might count such
experts on the fingers of one hand. And
among these five radium specialists how many
were capable of even diagnosing correctly
the exact cause of Prince Hohenhoff's or the
Duchess of Marister's blindness?

Sir Floyd Garston had already stated that
the Renwick case had given Beatrice Messonier a lead in the science of radium-therapy.
A host of medical journals had hurried the
eminent physician's statement into print.
So it was evident to the young detective
that the first seeds of the Tsarka conspiracy
were bearing fruit. He himself had been
caught and used as an advertising medium
for the Messonier Institute.

One hope shone through Gifford's far-reaching speculations — his faith in Beatrice Messonier's innocence of the stupendous designs so craftily engineered around her. It was her splendid art which promised to revolutionize modern surgery, and it was this fact which had caused Teroni Tsarka to create those very complaints which her genius promised to annihilate.

Gifford strode thoughtfully in the direction of Huntingdon Street, halting near the corner to allow a red landaulette car to rush past him. To his amazement the car stopped at the doors of the Radium Institute. A moment later the figure of Prince Hohenhoff descended, and was assisted through the wide entrance by his liveried chauffeurs.

"A royal bird to the net!" Gifford muttered as he waited for the prince to gain the consulting room.

Many of the morning papers had published an account of Prince Hohenhoff's career as a collector of art treasures and Japanese paintings, together with his portrait. Gifford's sympathies were touched by the young man's evident sufferings as he entered the white-panelled Institute supported by his chauffeurs. Already the terror of blindness had pinched his cheeks, leaving the mark of its fingers about his drawn lips and sunken chin.

After he had entered the Institute, Gifford retreated farther beyond the street angle, intending to interview Beatrice when the royal patient returned to his car. The Institute was overshadowed by a seven-story dental hospital opposite. A few carriages and motors passed in the direction of New Bond Street. Gifford, from his coign of vantage, became suddenly aware of a small feminine figure crossing the road from the hospital side. Heavily veiled and half-concealed in motor furs, Gifford had some difficulty in recognizing the slim, Madonna-faced Pepio Tsarka. But even her well-padded coat and her veil could hardly conceal her nationality. With a hesitating fear in each step her eyes searched to left and right as she approached the Institute. Then he became aware of a second approach to the Radium Institute as the daughter of the little nerve specialist slipped suddenly down a half-seen passage, on the east side of the building, and disappeared.

Gifford followed her down the passage and

saw the edge of her coat when she turned into a narrow court leading to the rear of the Institute. Soundless as a panther he was upon her while her yale key was opening a small, green-painted door in the wall.

She turned with a trembling cry, the key almost slipping from her fingers. A Japanese word escaped her that she had uttered when he lay blind and hurt in her father's house.

"Pepio Tsarka, what are you doing here?" he asked.

She raised her veil to look at him now, and her Asian eyes seemed to sob for mercy.

"May I ask," he repeated, "why you are seeking an entry into the rear of the Institute?"

"I came to consult Madame Messonier." The sobbing eyes did not meet his this time. "You see ——" she took off her glove quickly, holding out her slim, brown hand for his inspection. "I was playing with some horrible radium stuff, this morning, and the bulb broke. My fingers are sore and I was afraid to tell my father."

Her eyes sought his imploringly as he stooped to examine a peculiar stain on the tips of her fingers.

"Pepio Tsarka," he said without looking

up, "do you know that your friend, Soto Inouyiti, tried to kill me last night?"

"I saw it in the papers. Oh, the shame of it, the shame!" Her breath came in laboured efforts.

He regarded her shrewdly, the beautiful Japanese face and downcast eyes; and he thought of the boy, Inouyiti, who had fired twice in his direction, of the bull-necked Horubu, who had driven his steel-hipped car over the bodies of live men and women. It seemed monstrous, incredible, that this girl-child should be associated with a gang of human tigers. His blood leaped at the thought.

"Pepio," he said grimly, "I am going to have you detained!"

She gave a little scream that reminded him of a hurt child. He did not speak for a few seconds, the quiet sobbing disturbed him not a little.

"I am very sorry, Pepio; but your father's wicked operations must be checked."

"Why — why I know nothing!" she gasped. "Do you English punish women and girls because they are the children of ——"

"Say it!" he commanded.

"Of criminals?" she went on.   "Do you accuse me of my father's sins?"

"I do not accuse you of anything.   I want your father, Pepio.   It is my duty to have you arrested at sight."

A touch of regret came upon him as his fingers closed gently but firmly on her wrist. Yet, with Pepio in safe custody, her father might be levered into subjection. It was a bold stroke he was playing, but the welfare of innumerable lives depended upon her father's future operations.

"If you cry there will be a crowd," he warned her. "You will readily understand how awkward it is to have a daughter of Doctor Tsarka roaming the city unprotected," he added with a smile. "If once a London crowd detected your personality, or knew you for one of the people who drive steel-fronted cars over them, there would be an act of lynch law in Trafalgar Square."

Gifford talked to gain time. He was not quite certain of his next move. To ring up McFee of Scotland Yard and charge Pepio with complicity in the recent studio outrage would be unjust, criminal almost; for in his heart he knew that the sweet-mannered

Japanese girl was in no way concerned with the doings of her countrymen. It was his business to make war on those men, not on the women of their households. Yet he was not prepared to say how far he might venture under the circumstances. The Tsarka gang made war upon women and men alike, and it was only by striking at Pepio that he could hope to circumvent their activities.

She walked beside him into the street, where Prince Hohenhoff's car still waited outside the Institute. Gifford indicated it meaningly.

"Another of Inouyiti's victims. A gentleman who never harmed one of your kind."

The arms of the Hapsburgs, emblazoned on the red panels, caught Pepio's eye. She flushed instantly.

"I am so sorry, Mr. Renwick, so sorry!" was all she could say.

Gifford took her hand again, very gently, and scrutinized the stains on her fingers.

"Does your father allow you in his laboratory?" he asked, his glance playing round the tiny silver scar near her finger tips.

"Sometimes, when Horubu is not there," she answered without a tremor. "To-day

I went in while he was examining the model of a rubber finger."

"Oh!" Gifford released her hand; his lips twitched slightly. "What use would your father have for a rubber finger, Pepio?"

"The original belonged to Inouyiti. He carried radium in it until he lost it. My father is trying to make him another."

Gifford's heart softened at her unguarded manner. "Does your father allow you to play in his laboratory, Pepio, knowing it to be a dangerous place?"

"No; I went in to have a look at the finger model again while he was in the library. I came upon a glass bulb containing radium. It broke in my hands, and very foolishly I tried to collect the pieces."

Gifford was convinced of the truth of her statement. He marvelled, however, at the free and easy way Doctor Tsarka permitted her to pass to and from the City. A more astute criminal would have kept her in a close carriage rather than risk the chance of her being shadowed.

Something of his thoughts appeared to enter the young Japanese girl. She regarded him in tremulous anticipation.

"No one prevents me coming or going. My father thinks that I am known only to one detective — yourself."

"He thinks I am too chivalrous to arrest you, Pepio?"

"No and yes. He fancies that my eyes are sharper than yours," she answered with a sigh. "And yet, only yesterday, he told Horubu that you were a saimusir."

"What is a saimusir?" Gifford demanded with a blush.

"It is the Bushido equivalent for knight-errant, a man of ideals and gentle birth."

"And because your father regards me as a saimusir, Pepio, he thinks that you may wander with impunity under my very eyes?"

Gifford was nearer to anger than he cared to confess. To be considered a knight-errant by a master criminal was not flattering to his pride. The time had passed when even young detectives allowed the daughters of society terrors to go unshadowed.

A dozen paces from the Institute doors he paused, his arm still linked in Pepio's. A liveried attendant, the one who had carried his card to Beatrice Messonier, came out leisurely and spoke quietly to the Prince chauffeur.   Ten seconds later the red-panelled car sped from the street in the direction of Piccadilly.   The attendant returned to the steps of the Institute.

"The Prince has been detained.   Now, Pepio, you had better consult Beatrice about your radium scar.   Suppose we go in to-gether!"

Gifford drew her gently toward the white-columned portico, his lips tight set.   Pepio regarded him in innocent wonderment.

"Madame will consider it very unusual."

"I want to ask her a question in your presence, Pepio.   She is your father's servant. Am I right?"

They were on the steps of the Institute, and the carved figure of the Nazarene looked down at them from the wide entrance.   Some dormant instinct moved the young detective to uncover his head before the outstretched hands of Christ.   Pepio's fingers tightened on his arm as though she were afraid.

"If Beatrice Messonier is your father's servant she will not answer my question." He spoke in a half-whisper as though uncon-scious of her presence.

The liveried attendant came forward with

a curious smile of recognition as he took Gifford's card.

"Madame Messonier is engaged, Mr. Renwick. May I say that you will call again some hour this afternoon?"

"Madame will see my lady friend," ford retorted. "Miss Tsarka," he added coldly.

The attendant lingered a moment, on the order, breathing apologies. Much exercise up and down winding stairs had given edge to his temper.

"Madame Messonier is engaged," he insisted. "Your message must wait, sir."

"My message will wait until Prince Hohenhoff has been attended to — not a moment longer." Gifford spoke without heat as he drew Pepio into the white-panelled waiting room.

The attendant retired swiftly and without sound, leaving the young detective staring rather moodily at the grotesque carving above the high French windows.

A glance at his watch warned him that the hour of his appointment with Mrs. Cranstone was drawing near. She would come with her daughter to the Institute, he felt certain. There rose in him now a stern desire to challenge the mysterious power that guided the fortunes of the Radium Institute, a power which threatened to grind the last coin from its trembling victims.

It seemed ages before a sound reached him. The voice of Prince Hohenhoff was heard very faintly. Gifford strained forward to catch Beatrice's answer. At that moment the Hohenhoff car appeared at the door, as though the chauffeur had been secretly notified of the Prince's readiness to depart.

Leaning on the attendant's arm Prince Hohenhoff passed the waiting-room door and entered his car. Gifford rose with Pepio's hand in his and walked deliberately into the luxurious operating room which had been occupied by the royal visitor only a few moments before.

Beatrice Messonier was standing midway between the high-seated chair and the door. A look of depression, of exhausted effort, was upon her, as one who had recently flung her soul into the crucible of her science.

Only by the strange gentleness of gesture and pose would he have known her. She looked once at Pepio and then straight into his own fearless eyes.

"Why do you honour me with a visit, Mr. Renwick?" she asked simply. "People who have been blind rarely come back to my little theatre."

There was no mistaking the undercurrent of pain in her words. And Gifford remembered the day he had staggered into her operating chair when the fingers of the radium devils were striving to unseat his reason. He could not, however, subdue the overpowering impulse which had driven him to his self-allotted task.

"Madame Messonier," he began, with difficulty, "may I ask you a simple question relating to the general management of this Institute?"

He had expected his question to evoke some sign of mental perturbation, some shadow of annoyance or hesitation. Her answer was swift and startlingly direct.

"This Institute was organized by an old university associate of mine. At present it is entirely under my directorship."

"Entirely, Madame Messonier?"

She flushed slightly at his question.

"I speak in the sense of an ordinary house surgeon, Mr. Renwick. With its financial arrangements I have little or nothing to do."

"May I ask the name of the university associate you mentioned a moment ago?"

"You mean Dr. Teroni Tsarka. There is now no secret about the matter," she added innocently.

Gifford felt that Pepio was secretly quailing. He did not look at her as he again addressed Beatrice.

"You are aware, Madame Messonier," he went on, "of the recent attack on a party of art connoisseurs by a Japanese painter by the name of Soto Inouyiti."

"Prince Hohenhoff explained the circumstances a few minutes ago," she answered thoughtfully. "There were five or six victims, I understand."

Gifford pondered over her words, and then, in a slightly subdued voice, put another question.

"Are you aware that Soto Inouyiti, the young Japanese artist who perpetrated the iniquity, is a *protégé* of Doctor Tsarka?"

Her eyes flamed instantly, and then grew strangely cold.

"I think you are mistaken, Mr. Renwick," she said. "There cannot be the slightest truth in your statement."

Gifford felt the pressure of Pepio's fingers on his arm. He regarded her with a touch of pity.

"Will you tell Madame Messonier that I am speaking the truth?" he asked gently. "Will you tell her that Soto is your father's friend, and that only last night he attempted my life?"

Pepio inclined her head while a smothered sob escaped her.

Beatrice Messonier bent forward and shook the trembling Japanese girl by the shoulder. "Speak out, child! Were those people trapped in Soto's studio with your father's knowledge?"

"Soto is my father's friend," Pepio admitted faintly. "Do not judge him too harshly. He is only a boy. It was Horobu's fault, and," she paused as though the name almost stifled her, "my father's, too!"

All the life had gone from Beatrice's face. A great dejection came upon her, a weariness begotten of her patron's criminal duplicity. This, then, was the fame he had promised her! The healing of a group of incurable notabilities whose pain and distress were the result of his Machiavellian schemes!

Gifford was loath to tell the woman who had saved him from blindness that she was a party to an unprecedented infamy. The urgency of his mission cut his questions short.

"May I ask if the fees charged by the Institute are arranged by you?" he ventured at last.

"Not by me," she answered bleakly. "Yesterday," she waited a moment as though trying to regain her usual composure, "yesterday I read of the studio outrage in Piccadilly, and I was inclined to regard it as the result of an anarchist's plot, although the scientific manner of its arrangement set me thinking of ——"

"Doctor Tsarka," Gifford prompted.

"Yes, of Doctor Tsarka!" She passed slowly to the window overlooking the street, and the young detective saw a tear flash on the half-turned cheek.

"Now that we understand," he continued quietly, "I want to beg a favour of you in regard to Miss Violet Cranstone. You are aware, perhaps, that she is the fifth victim in the studio affair?"

"She came early this morning." Beatrice spoke with face to the window, and the effort of speech seemed to shake her. "She came this morning, and I was compelled to demand a certain fee. You will understand, Mr. Renwick, how sorry I am that any̱one should be refused treatment here."

Gifford bowed slightly. "Miss Cranstone will call at 12.30. Have I your assurance, Madame Messonier, that she will receive the same treatment which you accorded me?"

"I cannot promise until I have an opportunity of consulting my patron," was her unexpected answer.

"You mean Doctor Tsarka?"

"I shall mention no names, Mr. Renwick. You are a detective, and you have made accusations against Doctor Tsarka which affect me also. He was my friend and university associate in Tokyo. I cannot believe what you say is true!" she cried bitterly. "Some terrible mistake has happened."

Her eyes sought Pepio's for an instant, but the Japanese girl had covered her face as though to avoid meeting her glance.

Gifford understood the poignancy of her emotions, and he was loath to impose his will upon her at such a moment. But he was determined that Voilet Cranstone should

receive treatment at the Messonier Institute.
He could not allow a friendless young girl
to become the one victim of the Tsarka
combination. In forty-eight hours blindness
would overcome her, unless Beatrice consented
to operate.

He turned again to the set, white face of
the young radium specialist to make his
final appeal.

"I promised Mrs. Cranstone that you
would see her daughter. You understand,
Madame Messonier, that the young lady
entered the studio uninvited. She is too
poor to provide the fees of this institution.
You will not, as a Christian lady, allow her
to become blind. You have the power and
the skill," he added passionately, "and yet
you condemn a struggling artiste to a fate
worse than death, because ——"

The sudden flame in her eyes suspended
further utterance. Gifford breathed quickly,
as though conscious of the injustice of his
words.

"I beg your pardon, Madame Messonier,"
he said contritely. "I am not an experienced
advocate. The circumstances of this studio
infamy are likely to press upon one's nerves."

Beatrice Messonier turned away, and the effect of his words was not manifest. He dared not press her further. Any attempt at coercion would rebound on Violet Cranstone. It became increasingly evident that Beatrice was in some way dependent for advice upon the little Japanese doctor. She appeared unable to decide upon any point without his approval.

Bowing slightly, Gifford withdrew hastily from the Institute, with Pepio's arm in his. In the street he paused to consult his watch. It was nearly half-past eleven. Mrs. Cranstone would arrive at 12.30 sharp to experience, probably, another refusal for a consultation.

A telephone bureau stood at the opposite corner. Turning to Pepio, he indicated it briefly.

"Before I accomplish your arrest," he said slowly, "I want to ask your father a question."

"Do you want me to lead him into a trap, Mr. Renwick?" she flashed back.

He smiled at her reassuringly. "I have no intention of making you a decoy, Pepio Tsarka. I want you to beg for a life — yes, the very life of an innocent girl. He has the power to instruct Madame Messonier for good in this instance.   Will you ask him to allow Madame to operate on Miss Cranstone to-day?"

He felt the young Japanese girl tremble as he released her arm. "If your father and his people," he went on pleadingly, "intend to wage a war of medical blackmail against the rich of England and America, they will, I feel sure, spare the children of widows and struggling professionals."

A stifled sob escaped Pepio. She turned to cross the road and then looked back at him over her shoulder. He understood what was in her mind.

"I give you my word that I will not approach the bureau while you are inside," he called out.

Swiftly, and without a second glance in his direction, Pepio Tsarka entered the telephone bureau.

CHAPTER XIV

A SMALL white rat ran across the study table and perched meekly on Doctor Tsarka's outstretched hand. The loud ticking of a bronze clock over the book-covered shelf seemed to emphasize the terrible silence of the house.

Very tenderly the Japanese nerve specialist permitted his fingers to caress the smooth head of the inquisitive rodent as the pointed nose breathed over the gold cuff links inside his sleeve.

Satuma, the coolie servant, entered the study almost without sound to place a small decanter of wine at his master's elbow. He remained in the doorway for several moments before departing, as though expecting an order from the bent little figure in the chair.

The white rat, growing tired of its position on the outstretched hand, crept inside the open sleeve and fell asleep. Doctor Tsarka looked up slowly; the wine at his elbow seemed to indicate the coolie's presence in the study.

"Pepio San has not yet come home?" he said inquiringly. "Did you see her go out this morning, Satuma?"

"It has been the heaven of my existence to watch her come and go," the servant responded. "She left before the master came from his library this morning."

"Tsh! How can I read when Horubu may be in the hands of the police, or that young fool Inouyiti babbling to these English detectives in some suburban lock-up!"

The coolie bent his head in token of sorrow, but vouchsafed no reply. Doctor Tsarka stirred the sleeping rat in his sleeve tenderly while his thoughts wandered again to his truant daughter.

"Satuma," he said without looking up, "you must not allow Pepio San to enter the laboratory during my absence."

The servant trembled silently. "This morning," Doctor Tsarka continued, "my daughter broke a bulb containing several milligrammes of radium."

"Mine is the blame," the servant admitted cringingly. "Yet I cannot watch her always. Her feet are like gossamer. She makes no sound when she passes through the house."

"She is unlike most of her country-women in that respect," Tsarka muttered. "Still, the bulb was broken. . . . Do not let it happen again, Satuma, or you return to your rice-eating relatives in Tokyo. Atishan!"

The servant vanished without sound, leaving the little specialist brooding over a small leather bound volume at his elbow. But Doctor Tsarka was not deeply interested in the printed words before him; he was thinking of the wayward daughter over whose movements he had already lost control. Yet all his energies had been directed in the creating of wealth for her spending. Pepio was the last of his line; she was the one thing on earth that carried something of his spirit. His indulgent manner arose from his passionate devotion to this one surviving child. Without her his gigantic schemes for amassing wealth were futile speculations.

He would gladly have seen her married to Inouyiti, but since that impulsive young artist had allowed an English actress to steal his affections he put aside the thought for the present.

Day and night the fear of a police raid haunted him. Yet, of all the London criminal experts who were scouring the metropolis to locate his whereabouts, only one man had actually crossed the threshold of his house. He did not fear Renwick. There was too much of the dreamer in the young English-man to make him a formidable opponent. His sympathies were constantly betraying him.   In the hands of a pretty woman he was as malleable as gold.

Still, he thought it unwise for Pepio to venture abroad while Renwick was hunting for their present whereabouts.   Each fresh sound in the street outside caused him in-tolerable pangs.

The morning papers had given awesome details of Horubu's work overnight.   Eighteen men and women had been maimed and in-jured under the wheels of the iron car. Descriptions of Horubu and Inouyiti were appearing everywhere.   The *Times* had chron-icled Renwick's account of the rubber finger, together with its recovery by the two Jap-anese desperadoes outside the offices of the International Inquiry Bureau.

The empty car had been discovered near the Embankment, but, as yet, no traces of the radium stealers had come to the knowl-edge of Scotland Yard.

"Eighteen lives risked for six grains of radium — or three lives per grain, eh, Kezzio?" The little nerve specialist pinched the ears of the sleeping rat maliciously, drew it squeaking from his sleeve and permitted it to lie for an instant in his palm.

"What do you think of the radium blood-trail, my little magic worker? Men have died for gold, but this year they will slay and poison each other for the god in the pitchblende!"

Rising from his seat he turned into the passage and descended to the small laboratory situated in the basement of the house, where he worked generally during the earlier hours of the day. Kezzio, the white rat, found a comfortable bed near the warm furnace under the barred window.

He was grimly amused at the manner of Horubu's escape from the infuriated mob. The recovery of the lost radium would augment Beatrice Messonier's scant supply, and allow her to complete her operations.

A distant clock chimed the hour of midday. He paused with a magnesium wire held in the glowing beam of a "cathode ray" and listened intently.

The street door was unlocked and shut with unusual celerity. Heavy footsteps sounded in the outer passage. A minute later the laboratory door was thrust open; Horubu entered alone, his great coat pulled about his ears.

"It is raining, Teroni," he volunteered with a brief nod to the little figure stooping beside the "cathode ray." "An umbrella gives one a chance to hide one's face, eh?"

"Your face is one that the police are not likely to forget, Horubu. Where is the boy Inouyiti?"

"Gone to some hasheesh den to forget his sorrows. He is worried about this English actor girl. His shooting was worse than the Russians' at Dalny."

The ex-soldier threw his wet coat over a chair near the furnace, and stood for a moment watching the elf-like figure of Tsarka engrossed in his experiments.

"You do not congratulate me on my safe motor ride, Teroni." He spoke with a cynical gleam in his eyes. "You have seen the papers, too!"

Doctor Tsarka gazed at the bull-necked figure through a mist of molecular light, the muscles of his lips tight drawn.

"You acted with your usual courage, my dear friend. To have allowed that mob to stay you would have been disastrous to us. You put them in their proper place, Horubu."

The ex-soldier dropped into a chair, wiping the rain-drops from his ears.

"Some cars have a knack of killing men on their own account. The tumbril I drove at them coughed like a tiger when it caught a man on the run. Once a car has tasted blood, Teroni ——"

"You believe that?" The little nerve specialist put aside the magnesium wire and returned to the crucible.

Horubu wolfed the edges of a cigar hungrily, while the old bullet scar on his cheek showed livid in the afternoon light.

"I tell you I could not stop that old Manchurian car from grinding down the pale fat men who had assailed me. It jumped at them, zig, zig, zig, like that, my friend; it caught them in couples and in packs. It set me thinking, Teroni."

"Of what?"

"That a small body of Japanese could plunder this London, this city of bullion tanks." The ex-soldier buried his face in smoke fumes for a moment, his black thumb and forefinger plucking at his thin moustache. "Twenty thousand of our fellows could hold up the banks and strip the town."

"How would you get them into London?" Tsarka laughed.

"Have another exhibition next year or the year after. Pour your men into all the little ports. The officials would think of the exhibition every time a party of young Japanese gentlemen came off a ship. Tashan! Once in the city of London we could seize railways and telegraphs until we had stripped the banks."

Horubu smoked with his face to the laboratory furnace. Tsarka's mouth tightened again.

"How would you get these twenty thousand Jap soldiers out of the city," he asked quietly, "assuming that you were not instantly overwhelmed?"

Horubu shrugged. "It would not matter what happened to them if a dozen of us go away with some of John Bull's gold. We must not be too patriotic, my dear Doctor."

The little nerve specialist nodded some-

what wearily, as one who had long ago measured the man he had chosen to assist him
in his schemes of plunder.

"We are forgetting our position, Horubu,"
he remarked acidly.   "You have not yet
explained the result of your adventure."

Horubu moved with cat-like stealth in
his chair.   "Your mind is on the six grains
of radium, eh, Teroni, that I recovered from
Renwick outside Scotland Yard?"

"Where is it?" Doctor Tsarka leaned forward, his eyes scarce concealing his feverish
anxiety.

The ex-soldier tapped his pocket with unexpected insolence of manner.

"Valued at six thousand pounds, my dear
Teroni. The Berlin Radium Bank would
advance me its full value if I presented it.
Six thousand pounds, Teroni!   Think of
it!"

"We have no intention of selling it, Horubu.
It would be difficult to obtain fresh supplies
at present. And we are not in immediate
need of the cash. Give it to me. It is not
a good thing to carry in your pocket."

The ex-soldier smoked as though uncon-
scious of Tsarka's outstretched hand. His

great chest heaved slowly, as one suppressing an impromptu declaration.

"Give it to me, Horubu!" the Jap doctor insisted. "You do not quite understand its poisonous properties."

"I know that it will blind a man!" chuckled the ex-soldier, "or eat like leprosy into your blood. I know, too," he went on in gruffer tones, "that it will buy me a comfortable home in Osaka and half a score of house servants to attend me the rest of my life. I have fought Russians in their damnable trenches, suffered the horrors of frost-bite in Manchuria for a few pence a day. So . . . you must not be in a hurry to get back your six thousand pounds of poison, Teroni. You must let me hug your riches a little while longer. I have hungered and bled, you know!"

Doctor Tsarka recoiled from the slow-speaking comrade whose strength of purpose was equal to his own.

"You do not understand how urgently the radium is needed at the Institute, Horubu," he protested. "At any moment we may expect a message from Beatrice Messonier requesting more radium. We are on

the threshold of a great fortune, my friend —
twenty thousand pounds in a month if we are
prompt and skilful."

"It is a fool scheme through and through,"
the ex-soldier grunted. "Do you expect
this Duchess of Marister to pay Messonier a
five thousand guinea fee? Do you think
this German prince can meet your claims?
The police will raid the Institute, seize the
furniture, instruments, everything which has
cost us so much money."

Doctor Tsarka faced him with kindling
eyes. "After all, you are a man of fears,
Horubu. You have in you the little
child's terror of the policeman. You imagine
Scotland Yards and International Bureaus
to be controlled by supernatural people,
instead of a set of dull, unimaginative bores.
We have no criminal friends in England
likely to 'put us away.' We are self-centred
and bare-faced. One weak link is Inouyiti."

"Not Inouyiti, the Messonier woman,"
Horubu corrected sullenly. "Once she sus-
pects that you are supplying her with patients
she will spring at you like a tigress. She ——"

The laboratory telephone rang at Tsarka's
elbow. He turned sharply, as though the

sound had struck blade-like on his nerves.
Horubu frowned.

"This telephone is your fad, Teroni. We
could do without it. The police control it
at the central depots, I feel certain."

Tsarka gestured impatiently as he took
up the receiver. The lines about his mouth
hardened to a fierce smile with each word
that reached him.

Horubu, with colossal assurance, drew near
so that the message became audible to him.

"It is only Pepio." Doctor Tsarka spoke
in a slightly altered voice, as though resenting
the ex-soldier's inquisitive attitude. "You
are not interested in my daughter's affairs!"

Horubu did not change his listening posture.
Leaning his bull-head across the little table
he drank in each word that filtered across
the wires.

"I have been detained outside the Institute
by Gifford Renwick. He desires me to tell
you that unless Miss Cranstone receives
special attention at the hands of Beatrice
Messonier, without fees of any kind, he will
charge me with complicity in the studio
outrage."

The message came in Japanese, but each

word played like a scythe on Teroni Tsarka's nerves.

Horubu laughed hoarsely. "The stupid Englishman has got your heart in his hand, my dear Doctor, just as Nogi had Stoessel's at Port Arthur. His teeth are in your loins, and you are going to squeal," he added brutally.

The little nerve specialist remained stooping forward, the receiver held close to his ear.

"Are you speaking from a police station, Pepio?" he asked without a tremor.

"From the bureau at the corner of Huntingdon Street. Mr. Renwick is waiting outside."

Tsarka answered in the same unemotional voice. "My life is in your hands, Pepio. If you give Mr. Renwick this address we must surrender to the police."

"He has not demanded it," was Pepio's answer. "Mr. Renwick is a gentleman. He uses no threats. He only desires you to save Violet Cranstone."

Horubu drew away from the telephone as a tiger moves from its feasting place. Doctor Tsarka watched him curiously.

"What do you think of it?" he asked.

The light of battle was in Horubu's eyes; his muscle-packed hands flashed up and out in quick gestures of anger and surprise.

"Your pretty daughter has pitched us into the lap of the police. We are asked to surrender."

"A small fee," Tsarka interjected.

"Two thousand guineas. The Cranstones would pay at a pinch. Renwick has fallen on your communications. Fight him now or our position becomes untenable!"

"The Marister-Hohenhoff fees will be due in a day or two, at least. They may have paid Beatrice her fees — ten thousand or more. Renwick is evidently moved to compassion for this comedy actress. Let us placate him now. To-morrow I will force the Duchess of Marister to pay by cheque. Trust me, Horubu."

He paused, breathless almost, to consult a shipping register at his elbow, his finger seeking out the dates of sailing.

"To-morrow is Friday, Horubu," he went on hurriedly. "In six days we shall be safely in New York. Let me promise this Renwick that the Cranstone girl shall be accorded free treatment at the Institute."

"I promise nothing!" came from the ex-soldier. "Do you think that Renwick will let us alone when he finds that he can strike at our lungs! Pepio knows nothing of our financial interest in the Messonier Institute. The Messonier herself cannot trace the Inouyiti affair to us. She does not know the boy. Deny everything. Make the comedy actress pay with the others — she will find the money. Force Renwick to some more fighting. Try the faith of your Beatrice, but, above all, my dear Doctor, no surrender!"

The words came in tones of broken thunder from the ex-soldier, his swart, heavy features appeared to congest under the strain of his emotions.

Tsarka's hand trembled on the receiver, and then grew steady.

"Then Pepio goes to prison!" he said humbly. "Is that your wish, Horubu?"

"I do not wish it!" the ex-soldier retorted. "But if women thrust themselves into the fighting line, they must suffer at the hands of the enemy."

CHAPTER XV

WITHOUT a glance at the ex-soldier Doctor Tsarka spoke into the tube: "Tell Mr. Renwick that I will use my influence to enable Miss Cranstone to receive instant treatment. Are you listening, Pepio?"

"Yes, my father. We are waiting for Miss Cranstone's arrival. She is late; but if you send a wire to madame at once there will be time."

Tsarka put away the receiver, scrawled a note on a piece of paper, and approached the laboratory door. Satuma appeared at his first call, and departed hurriedly with the note on the nearest telegraph office. The Jap doctor closed the laboratory door and returned to his place near the furnace.

Horubu scowled as he walked past, but the ex-soldier's glances were lost on Tsarka. He was thinking of his dark-eyed daughter who had imperilled her liberty and his own. He did not enjoy opposing Horubu, but he felt instinctively that he was pursuing a safe course in temporarily placating Gifford Renwick. He was also certain that the young detective would not carry out his threat to arrest Pepio.

He stared dully at the squat figure of Horubu, the ham-shaped fists and swollen neck, and again reiterated the question so vital to their interests.

"You are forgetting the radium, comrade. I must have it now. Life is short; we waste the precious hours in argument. Will you deliver the radium to me?"

"No, my dear Doctor, I shall retain it as my share of the loot. It will buy me a very comfortable villa in Osaka or somewhere on the Pacific slope. Do not bother me further with your plans. I have gone out of the business."

"Give me three grains, Horubu, a one-half of the whole. It is all mine by right. Did I not drag it from the wash pipes of Professor Moritz's laboratory? Give me three grains and go your way."

Tsarka made his appeal without a gesture, for he knew that the bullet-headed campaigner could not be moved by threats or promises.

Robbed of his radium supply his life would end in poverty and disaster.

A sudden hatred of this close-fisted *confrère* seized him, yet a certain fear of his tigerish strength held Tsarka's passion in check.

"I am very sorry, my dear Horubu, that we do not agree upon these little affairs. Your services in the past have been invaluable. I do not blame you for trying to recoup yourself."

The little Jap doctor sighed wearily, as he turned again to his crucible.

Horubu sat immovable in the chair, save for the occasional lifting of a tobacco-stained forefinger to trim the ash of his cigar. The afternoon shadows lengthened perceptibly across the high-walled yard. In the room overhead they heard a soft, chanting note as one of the coolie servants plied his soft broom over the carpeted floor.

Tsarka, standing by the furnace, watched the orange-hued mass of ever-changing mineral compounds in the glowing crucible, stirring it softly from, time to time with a long iron ladle. In the past Horubu had been accustomed to sit and watch him refining and testing his strange metals and chemical fluids, until his curiosity in laboratory work had grown dull.

Tsarka looked up from the furnace and saw that the creeping shadows had enveloped Horubu's squat outline. The laboratory possessed only one large window, and the chirping of the house sparrows in the yard outside marked the gloomy afternoon silence.

"Since you do not intend to return the radium to me, Horubu, I presume that you will stay in England longer?"

Tsarka cast a handful of snow-white powder into the crucible, peering down as he did so to mark its effect on the molten mass within.

"It is a pity," he said, with an upward glance at the huge bulk in the chair, "that you cannot make up your mind about the radium."

Horubu stirred animal-like, his elephantine shoulders bulging from the shadow.

"You are repeating your demands with the tongue of a coolie woman, Teroni. You cannot sway me. My mind is fixed. . . ."

He stooped forward as though hypnotised by the sudden light in the nerve specialist's eye.

"What — what are you doing with that ladle, Teroni?"

Tsarka had stooped over the crucible and had drawn out a ladleful of the orange-coloured mass. Some of it dripped back into the crucible in fiery drops.

"What are you doing with that metal stuff?" Horubu had gained his feet with the celerity of a baited wolf, his slant eyes dilating with terror.

Tsarka turned like a priest upon the altar, and the smoke of his brimming ladle drifted in sulphurous gusts across the low-roofed laboratory. Horubu crouched back half a pace, and his heavy service revolver showed steel white in the ruddy flare.

"Tashan! You little dog!"

His bullet whanged against the window bar above the smoking ladle. Then a prismatic sheet of fire slashed through the air as the uplifted ladle shot outward. The scalding mass struck Horubu full on the brow. A roar of pain escaped him, that subsided into a snarl as he sought to brush away the molten drops from his hair and eyes.

Tsarka remained near the furnace, his swart face illumined by the up-shooting flames below.

"You are not a finished duellist, Horubu," he ventured, with a sudden gleam of savage irony. "You do not face the music like the ancient gentlemen of Japan."

A smell of scorching cloth filled the laboratory. All around where the ex-soldier lay the floor was covered with fiery pools of metal that turned to ghouts of colour in the cooling draught.

The pattering of sandalled feet outside roused Tsarka from his brooding survey of the laboratory floor. Satuma, who had returned after dispatching the telegram to Beatrice Messonier, peeped in at the door, his face alive with curiosity and wonder.

"Soto Inouyiti has come!" he called out. "He is drunk with wine, oh, master, and very violent! How shall I tell him that ——"

He paused, his alert eyes fixed on the groaning figure of Horubu huddled among the scalding pools of metal.

Tsarka leaned on the iron ladle, and his brow cleared. "Horubu has met with an accident, Satuma. Tell Inouyiti I will see him in a little while. Put him to bed. He is not very strong."

Satuma gasped; even his Japanese frigidity

thawed at sight of the groaning figure of the ex-soldier.

A word from Tsarka sent him hurriedly upstairs to attend the rebellious boy artist, whose unexpected return threatened to bring the police into the house.

Horubu raised himself to his elbow, his hands pressed to his face.

"Give me something to stop this pain. It was not good fighting to play such a trick, Teroni. Help me! This is not a pain to bear. Even a soldier must cry out!"

Tsarka peered at the seared face — livid where the whips of molten metal had struck. A touch of pity came upon him, for it was not a deep-seated hatred which had driven him to his terrible act. Horubu had been a willing worker in the past. It was greed that caused his undoing — a silly desire to wreck the labour of years. . . .

"I am sorry for you, comrade," he said with true Japanese affection. "There is a grain of human devilry in both our temperaments."

Horubu sought to gain his knees, his revolver still clutched in his right fist. "Take me somewhere into the light!" he choked.

"Send me to an hospital. Tashan; my face is burnt away. Help me, Teroni!"

"Put down your weapon, Horubu. Then . . . I will place a liniment on your face. The weapon ——"

A heart-shaking explosion smothered his words. Tsarka flinched as the bullet sobbed past his throat. Horubu, leaning on his elbow, listened with the air of a huntsman uncertain of his kill.

Doctor Tsarka remained perfectly still, as one counting his own heart-beats. He waited for the weapon to slant again in his direction, feeling sure that Horubu was guessing his aim.

"Teroni!" The ex-soldier crept half a foot nearer. "That shot was an accident, I swear by the gods! Where are you? Take this accursed pistol away; my hands are shaking with pain. I have no control . . ."

"If you stir a hand, Horubu, I will spill these red minerals on your stupid head!"

He lowered the brimming ladle until the lava-like heat smote the tortured face. "The Gehenna of the Chinaman smells no sweeter, eh, Horubu?" he added grimly.

A lion-like grunt was the only response.

The revolver fell to the laboratory floor, and Tsarka kicked it contemptuously into the far corner.

"Give me the radium," he said almost sharply. "Which pocket . . . your clothes are burning. Quick! You do not know what may happen!"

He knew enough of the ex-soldier's strength not to venture within arm's grip. An unknown fear of Horubu's lion-courage entered him as he viewed the mineral-scorched fists and clothes.

Slowly, painfully, Horubu fumbled at his pocket and drew out a fired blackened chocolate box. A smell of burning rubber struck upon Tsarka's senses.

Snatching the box from the outstretched hand his fingers touched a soft, sticky substance at the bottom.

"The radium is not here!" he snapped. "The fire has melted the rubber finger. But there is no radium!"

"The devil has it then!" Horubu groaned. "Asio! It was there when I came in here."

The little nerve specialist carried the warm rubber pulp to the window-light and examined it minutely through a lense. If the radium

had become coated with the fire-heated rubber
the application of a certain chemical solution
would reveal its presence instantly.

Taking a bottle from a near shelf he emptied its contents into a saucer, adding a few
grains of cyanide of potassium from a small
jar. Placing the rubber pulp into the saucer
he washed and sifted it with the craft of a
born analyst.

The elements of radium were as much a
mystery to him as to the average scientist,
but he knew that the dissolving rubber would
leave some trace of the precious substance
in the sedimentary deposit.

There was none.

He straightened his narrow shoulders with
an effort, and stared at the groaning figure
on the floor.

"You have lied to me, Horubu!" he called
out. "Your tongue is hot with falsehoods. A
beetle has stolen your honour. Thou fool!"

The ex-soldier crawled a few paces on his
chest and knees, his mutilated features revealed in the faint afternoon light. His groans
ceased as he turned in Tsarka's direction.

"I was fooled by a Jew, Teroni. Do not
strike with that fire until I have spoken."

He paused, his fingers pressing the white fire-blaze that stood like a Hindu caste-mark on his brow. "I have played the cheat, Teroni, and I have been made to swallow the accursed dregs of your crucible. Even the flesh of a samurai is not sacred from your chemical poisons!"

"Be swift with your remaining lies, O beetle brain!" snarled the Jap doctor. "I will not listen to your deceitful tongue. Where is the radium?"

"A Jew has it, Teroni. To-day I was to get four thousand pounds for it. I have his letter of acknowledgment in my pocket. His name is Paul Isaacson. His office is in Hatton Garden. I was sick of your fool's play, Teroni, and the chance came to be rid of you, so . . . I bargained with Paul Isaacson. . . ."

Horubu lay forward on his great chest, the sweat of torment streaming from his bull-throat. Behind him, on the laboratory floor, lay the fast cooling lake of metal which had seared and blinded him. But now that all hope of life had gone, his soldier's courage sat like a lion within him.

"I dreamed of a little house in my native

land," he went on, "and for that I drove the iron-car at the pig-headed London crowd. I wanted to go home to Osaka . . . to see my three sons. I was a fool to come here to-day . . . into this jehannum of fire and death!"

He stretched forward a piece of paper in his hand. "Take it, Teroni; it is Paul Isaacson's promise to pay the four thousand pounds. Give me a drink now."

Tsarka took the paper and scanned it cautiously. It became clear to him that the Hatton Garden Jew had bargained to make two thousand from the deal. His suspicious glance wandered from Isaacson's note of acceptance to the shape lying at his feet.

"Why did you come here to-day?" he demanded. "There was no need to see me again, Horubu, if you intended selling the radium."

"I left a little money in a cupboard up-stairs," the ex-soldier admitted. "Twenty sovereigns. There were other little things I wished to get. The picture of my wife, painted from a portrait by Inouyiti. That was all. I was so sure of my strength if it

came to blows with us, Teroni. I came to
brag of my deeds, and now my head is a
charred bone, and death is slow to come."

He lay on his face, and the long shadows
came to hide his torment from Teroni Tsarka.
Above, in one of the unoccupied rooms, the
voice of Inouyiti was heard singing a song of
wine and art interspersed with allusions to
certain ladies of France and Spain. He
paused at times, in his musical rhapsodies,
to hammer the table with his fists, because
the slow-footed Satuma had not returned with
the champagne he had promised to bring.

Later, the boy artist broke into loud lamen-
tations in which the name of the young
comedy actress, Violet Cranstone, was heard.
Doctor Tsarka listened, an acute sense of
tragedy overwhelming his mind and body.
Materialist though he was, he could not
resist the wave of superstitious awe that
threatened to grip him. Butoni, the Italian
scientist, had declared that radium was
impregnated with the power of God. Tsarka
was inclined to the belief that it contained
also the powers attributed to the Evil One.

The six grains of pure radium that he had
filched from the laboratory of Professor

Moritz only a few months before had caused a tiny maelstrom of terror to whirl through London. By its aid, Gifford Renwick, a student of criminology, had been trapped and rendered helpless for many weeks. Four wealthy art patrons had been inveigled into a studio and mercilessly tortured. His daughter, Pepio, had fallen into the clutches of the radium-god, and the train of mischance which had set her curious fingers searching his laboratory, for things to play with, had delivered her into the hands of Renwick. Horubu's maladroitness had set the seal of terror on the restored radium *cache*. Eighteen men and women had been ground and pulped beneath the wheels of his car. . . .

And now, when the last series of difficulties appeared to have vanished, Horubu had played him false, bringing into the scheme of things a Hebrew radium dealer named Paul Isaacson!

Stepping from his place near the furnace, Tsarka took a bottle of liniment from the shelf and stooped over the supine figure of the ex-soldier. Very tenderly he dressed the fire-blistered brow and eyes, bandaging the head with deftness and skill.

Horubu appeared to have fallen into a state of lethargy, moaning feverishly from time to time as the adroit fingers pressed the lint about his pulsating brows.

A touch of the electric button brought the coolie servant, and together they placed the metal-scarred ex-soldier on his own driving coat in a far corner of the laboratory.

Tsarka returned to his study somewhat shaken and indisposed after his terrible conflict. For once in life he yearned to lie beside his mutilated comrade and sleep forever. It was only the shadow of his old ambition that kept his heart alive now. There was Pepio, to be sure, and the little drunken Inouyiti whose whole thoughts were centred in another woman's pain.

Somewhere, he knew not where, he had heard a man say that he who lived by the sword should perish by the sword. Surely the same doctrine applied to the experimenters in modern chemistry.

An unmistakable tap, tap at the study door aroused him from his brooding lethargy. Satuma's face peered in at the door.

"A lady has come, O master!" he whispered. "She is waiting in the hall."

Tsarka's eyes grew wide with astonishment. "Who — who is she?" he demanded. "Does she inquire for me or Horubu?"

"The name Messonier," almost babbled the coolie. "I do not know her, O master!"

Tsarka slipped across the study, his left hand clenched against his brow.

"Show madame in here, Satuma. I did not hear you open the street door to let her in," he complained.

A mirror above the fireplace revealed his disordered attire, his smoke-blurred eyes and pain-drawn features. He did not wish Beatrice to see him at a disadvantage. These highly strung women had singular predilections for well-groomed men. A frock coat and spotless linen were expected of a student of chemistry, even though he were conducting an experiment with pitchblende and charcoal.

She was standing in the doorway watching his almost frantic efforts to straighten his faded cravat. He grimaced rather wearily as her reflection in the mirror became silhouetted against his own.

"My vanity needs a little chastisement,

Beatrice," he said at last. "I have been in the smoke where the million-eyed moleculars are born. The furnace burned not too clearly to-day."

She did not speak, and he knew by the shape of her mouth that calamity was lapping the foundations of the Institute.

"Pepio left here this morning," he went on like one anxious to evade some terrible indictment. "She causes me much uneasiness. My mind is not free to work."

Beatrice sighed, and he waited with simulated courtesy for her to speak.

"Pepio came to the Institute this morning, Doctor Tsarka, accompanied by Mr. Renwick."

"That Quixotic fool!" The little nerve specialist indicated a chair with an unconscious salaam. "I fear that his encounter with Horubu, in my laboratory, has affected his reason, Beatrice. You know that the radium inundated his nerve channels pretty freely?"

"Mr. Renwick is very sane at present, Doctor Tsarka; although," she paused, seemingly to loosen the button of her glove, "although his statements concerning that studio horror sounded unreal to me at first."

Satuma lit the lamp noiselessly, his slant eyes peering furtively at the beautiful white lady who had entered unbidden into the house of Horubu, the wolf.

Without sign or word she tactically declined to be seated. Something of the nervous irritation in her eyes warned Tsarka of impending hostilities. He retreated to his chair, as though driven to some point of refuge where his shaking limbs would not betray him.

His pain-stricken eyes held her dumb for an instant. She remembered her university days, his heaven-born guidance at a time when her soul and brain were in conflict with Titanic problems. . . . She could not judge him until he had spoken. He addressed her at last, and the old fire in his eyes kindled at each word.

"Renwick bears me no great love, Beatrice. You remember how he invaded my private hospital in Westmoreland Street under a very silly pretext. To-day he is begging a little gratuitous treatment for a poor young actress."

"I saw her at midday," Beatrice inclined her head. "Her position was indeed pathetic!"

"You treated her, of course?"

"I was not a moment too soon. A few more hours' delay and her case would have defied treatment." Beatrice paused, and then put a question upon which her whole future hung.

"Who is Soto Inouyiti?" she asked.

"A Japanese fanatic who has been sent to me for treatment. The poor boy is quite insane."

"You are sheltering him from the police?"

"When he is quite cured I shall hand him over to the authorities. Renwick seems to have made a great deal out of the studio affair. Inouyiti has been unsound of mind for a considerable period. He has a mother and father in Tokyo. I am afraid he will never see them again."

The mind of Beatrice Messonier oscillated between faith and unbelief. She had only known Teroni Tsarka as a kindly little specialist, whose sympathy and advice had lightened the bitterest months of her life. He did not impress her as a fugitive from justice.

The London doctors were no doubt eager to be rid of him, just as the people of her own profession had sought to snub and humiliate her.

Something of her wavering was manifest in her softening features. Tsarka drew himself together for his final appeal. He divined in a flash that she had come to resign her position.

"I admit that a series of accidents have occurred which put thousands of Japanese residents in London under suspicion. Inouyiti has been guilty of a foolish crime."

"And Mr. Renwick was nearly murdered into the bargain," she volunteered.

"I am not responsible for private vendettas, my dear Beatrice. Consider his original offence in entering my house upon a trumped-up charge. He was one of the first to enter Inouyiti's studio after that deplorable stereoscope incident, and while there he appropriated six grains of pure radium which Inouyiti had stolen from my laboratory."

"Was it to recover the radium that Horubu attacked him outside the International Bureau?" Beatrice wavered perceptibly.

"It may have been. I do not know much of Horubu. He is an old Manchurian war veteran who runs amok occasionally — the result, I fancy, of a head wound received at Liaoyang. I trust that the police will get him before long."

Beatrice was silent, feeling that, after all, she had judged her old master too hastily. Gifford Renwick had accused him of the most malignant offence conceivable, and she breathed a little easier at the manner of its refutal.

Tsarka rose from his seat, his old assurance manifesting itself in his tricks of speech and gesture.

"As to the financial aspect of the Institute," he went on, "we may soon be in a position to fight down the calumnies of our foes. Tell me, my dear Beatrice, have the Duchess of Marister and Prince Hohenhoff contributed their fees?"

The question came like a drop of oil from his lips; yet in his eyes there lived a torment of suspense that almost betrayed him.

"The Duchess presents her cheque for five thousand guineas to-morrow at midday. It is an incredible sum," Beatrice added with a burning cheek.

Tsarka shrugged good-humouredly. "Consider her station, my dear Beatrice. In one night we have ourselves been deprived of a similar amount by the loss of our radium. Prince Hohenhoff's fee is also due to-morrow?" he prompted delicately.

The flush in her cheeks attracted his shrewd glance.

"Prince Hohenhoff is considered the handsomest man in the German Legation," he ventured, with a sigh. "I trust that *his* case is progressing favourably."

"Very favourably. He is the least injured of any. I understand that although he is connected with one of the reigning sovereigns of Europe, his financial position scarcely merits our enormous demands upon his purse."

A flash of anger almost escaped the Japanese doctor. He recovered himself instantly.

"It is the way with German princes, my dear Beatrice. They are the beggars of society, the parasites on the parvenues' purse-strings."

The study door opened stealthily. Inouyiti, his face still bearing evidence of his recent adventures, stood swaying on the threshold.

CHAPTER XVI

MUCH wine had made the Japanese artist reckless. His ride with Ho-rubu through the screaming mob, outside the International Inquiry Bureau, had shaken nerve and brain until his reason trembled. Physically he was a handsome boy, with soft, brown skin and eyes. Unlike most Japanese youths his face lacked the broad Mongolian cheek-bone, the Simian brow and lips.

The sight of Beatrice Messonier steadied him just as a beautiful image or flower arrests the eye of a frenzied child. Tsarka's hand clutched savagely at a bell, near his elbow, as though he would hurl it at the intruder's head.

The panting figure of Satuma appeared instantly in the passage outside, sweat and anger in his baffled eyes. Tsarka cut short his meaningless apology.

"Take this patient from my study, Satuma, before his babblings drive me mad. Get him to his room!"

Inouyiti waved the coolie servant aside. "Keep those fingers for your master's throat, Satuma," he said defiantly. "And you, too, Teroni, remember that a policeman walks past here each evening at this hour."

"Your pulse is high, Inouyiti," Tsarka spoke with some restraint. "Be good enough to retire with my servant. You are sorry for your intrusion already. Japanese gentlemen are careful of their dignity in the presence of ladies."

Beatrice could hardly bring herself to believe that this tender-eyed boy artist was responsible for the most infamous outrage within memory. That his sudden entry had disconcerted Doctor Tsarka she easily divined, notwithstanding the little doctor's attempts to act with toleration and reserve.

Inouyiti bowed with excessive courtesy to Beatrice Messonier as he slipped past with the intention of confronting his one-time colleague.

"I must salute you, Teroni Tsarka, as the most accomplished impostor of the century. This lady," he again bowed to the spellbound Beatrice, "is Madame Messonier,

of whom we have heard so much.   It is well
that she should hear what I have to say."

"Peace, little fool, peace!" Tsarka remon-
strated.   "You, Satuma," he beckoned 'the
coolie servant sharply.   "See this patient
to his room, and do not allow him to again
intrude upon my privacy."

"I repeat that you are a colossal fraud,
Teroni, in the presence of this lady I repeat
it!"   Inouyiti shook the coolie's hand from his
shoulder and, with a cat-like spring, gained
the far end of the study, his hand resting
against the panel.

For an instant Tsarka mistook the levelled
hand for a loaded weapon.   He stooped like
one in fear of a bullet.

Inouyiti laughed hilariously.   "You squint
at death, Teroni; you cannot look it in the
face.   And the lady watching us both!"

"I am not afraid of death," Tsarka responded, "when it comes from a soldier or a
gentleman.   I object, however, to die at the
hands of an epileptic!"

The retort steadied the boy artist as a
whip-cut sobers a frolicsome panther cub.
Yet the resolve to expose his old mentor grew
fiercer each moment.   Duped, ruined, com-

pelled to hide from the eyes of the world, he turned upon the man who had wrought his downfall.   Not even the presence of Beatrice could stay his wild outburst.   His words poured in disjointed sentences over the quailing nerve specialist, lapsing occasionally into his native tongue when the passionate idioms failed to find expression in English.

"You promised me fame, Teroni, as you promised it to this lady.   People would worship my art; ladies would kneel at my feet. You lent me money, like a Jew, at interest, and you demanded my life in return.   It was Horubu and yourself who planned that bit of devil's work in my atelier . . .   Who fixed the molecular shower that turned the German baron into a spotted fool?   Who arranged the stereoscope lenses so that the radium sponge should press over the eyes of Prince Hohenhoff and blind him?"

Beatrice shrank farther into the shadow of the door from the terrible impact of words flung out with measured emphasis.   Inouyiti was no longer the incoherent babbler; each moment saw him steadier of eye and limb, until his denunciations reached the plane of a skilled prosecutor's.

He turned from the dismayed little doctor and addressed Beatrice in a strangely altered voice.

"Three years ago, madame, I lived with my parents in Tokyo. I painted fans and screens, selling them to the curio dealers for the price of a little food for my brothers and sisters. One of my sisters was ill of consumption; two of my brothers were shot at Dalny. It remained for me to help my mother and the little brothers who cried for more food in the terrible winter that came after the war.

"One day an American gentleman came to my studio and admired my pictures. He gave me a thousand dollars for two pictures and a small collection of fans. He advised me to go to London or New York, where I would become speedily famous. I came, and met Teroni Tsarka. You know something of the result of our friendship. . . . Last night he and his associate, Horubu, forced me under threats to attempt the life of a young Englishman named Renwick. I failed, and was compelled to sit in an iron car while it was driven through a crowd of indignant citizens. This morning," he continued passionately, "I learned from a newspaper that

Miss Cranstone had been refused treatment at the Institute because of her inability to pay a scandalous fee!"

Beatrice was about to speak; he stopped her swiftly, his eyes fixed on the palpitating nerve specialist.

"It was not your wish that Miss Cranstone should be turned away. Ask yourself from whence came the order to squeeze the last shilling from Prince Hohenhoff and the Duchess of Marister!"

Tsarka interrupted with a gust of laughter. "You almost convince me that I am a monster and a blackguard, Inouyiti. Still, I do not wish to defend myself from the attacks of a criminal degenerate. To-morrow, if Madame Messonier desires further proof of my words, we will call in a brain specialist to confirm my verdict that you are the victim of mental hallucinations. As for the heavy fees charged by the Institute over which madame presides," he went on with growing assurance, "we must demand them or retire from our profession. We are not dealing in ointments or cheap salves," he affirmed with a touch of pride, "but with radium — the costliest of known elements."

Beatrice made no response. Her destiny had been merged into the fortunes of Tsarka. No one else had offered to help her in the past. Yet Inouyiti's story moved her almost to tears. His manner was certainly strange, and in his pitiful little story she detected something of her own.

Inouyiti settled himself in a chair with a measure of defiance in his attitude. Tsarka's one hope lay in Beatrice's good-will. Once his fingers closed on the Marister-Hohenhoff fees he would escape with Pepio to America.

He talked volubly to Beatrice, ignoring the fiery-eyed boy artist who sat in Horubu's chair. The newspapers were beginning already to comment favourably on the improved condition of Prince Hohenhoff and the Duchess. At his signal the attendant produced an evening journal from the rack in the hall. Holding it near, he pointed to a cross-headed paragraph exultantly.

"Here are evidences of your growing fame, my dear pupil. See where your name shines at the head of the social column as the classic specialist of the century. That is very flattering, is it not!" he cried, observing the

heightening colour on her cheek.   "And this!"
he went on, indicating another paragraph.

"The Latest Miracle in Radio-Active Surgery.   Triumph of the New School Over the
Old.   Madame Messonier Restores the Hopelessly Blind."

Beatrice could not suppress a wild thrill
at the mention of her name in connection
with her recent successful operations.   The
journal from which Doctor Tsarka had quoted
was a high-toned publication, and severely
conservative in its social announcements.

"By the next mail we shall be deluged with
Continental press notices — French, German,
Italian.   The name Messonier shall ring
throughout the medical world."

Tsarka paced the study conscious that his
well-timed appeal to her vanity had neutral-
ized the effects of Inouyiti's *dénouément*.
She was reading the paper, her beautiful
features silhouetted in the lamp glow, her
eyes illumined by the first breath of journal-
istic praise.

Inouyiti watched her also, and the tragedy
of his own defeat put a new sting in his words.

"Only a week ago, madame, a leading paper
called me the Japanese Turner.   Another said

that my work rivalled Corot's.   To-day I am
hiding from the police.   I have warned you.
Beware of Tsarka's nets, or he may haul you
to your destruction!"

"Do not heed him," whispered Tsarka.
"He will sleep after you have gone; poor boy!"

Beatrice was now convinced of Inouyiti's
partial insanity.   Her mind was too pre-
occupied in her work to retain for long the
bitter outpourings of a disappointed genius.
She felt how unjust it would be to waste her
energies in proving Tsarka's honesty of purpose.   Her domain was the surgery, not the
investigation bureau.   Let Gifford Renwick
prove his allegations, she would return to
the Institute to complete the cure of Prince
Hohenhoff and the other victims of Inouyiti's
aboriginal impulse.

Muffled in his great motor coat, Doctor
Tsarka escorted her to the station, impressing
her, as they walked along the quiet streets,
with the need of continued study.

"We must work and study, my dear pupil,
in the teeth of calumny and disaster.   Be sure
that our enemies will not allow us a clear
field until we have demolished their ancient
theories.   Work, work!"

The train bore her to the City, and he returned by a circuitous route to the house. The night sounds alarmed him horribly; every column of shadow concealed the form of a police officer. Slamming doors caused him to leap round in a sweat of fear, expecting the hand of Renwick to close on his wrist and throat.

He gained the house, perspiration dripping from his brow. Satuma was waiting in the doorway to assist him with his muffler and great coat.

Entering the study, he drank a little wine to steady his tottering limbs. Inouyiti still occupied Horubu's chair. His head nodded drowsily; his lips twitched as the shadow of the little doctor fell goblin-like across the panel.

"More wine, Satuma, and then to bed!" Tsarka thrust the empty decanter across the table.

"But this mad boy, and Horubu downstairs in the laboratory?" the servant questioned.

"Horubu is not well. Do not go near the laboratory. He is comfortable for the present, Satuma. He is a heavy man to carry upstairs."

Inouyiti's eyes shone through the nimbus of gathering sleep.

"Horubu! I did not think he had returned!" He struggled to an upright position.

"Peace, child of the devil. Let me think. Your tongue has done enough work. The gods may split it yet. . . ."

A limp inertia had succeeded the young artist's passionate declarations. Fear begotten of his rashness stole upon him. Without sound or gesture he sat in the big-backed chair until Satuma returned with the wine. Then he lay back and watched Tsarka's process of nerve rehabilitation.

A yellow powder was dropped into the decanter, and the wine became instantly alive with curious meteor-like bubbles, that flashed and exploded their crimson gouts of scarlet into the purple wine.

Tsarka drank greedily from the decanter as though unable to control his aching thirst. Flushed under the eyes, but steadier of hand and limb, he sank contentedly into a chair opposite the quailing boy artist.

Satuma cleared the table of loose papers and then, with a profound salaam in Tsarka's direction, retired for the night.

Tsarka's mental outlook cleared instantly. With the Duchess of Marister's cheque for five thousand guinies in his possession nothing mattered. Renwick would not prosecute Pepio. There was not a scrap of evidence to show that she was in any way connected with the studio atrocity.

His chief annoyance now was Inouyiti. At any moment he was likely to surrender himself to the police and thereby bring about his instant arrest.

Tsarka lit a cigarette and pushed the wine decanter toward the brooding boy artist.

"You have been a fool, Soto. In your eighteenth year you imagine that the earth and sun no longer exist because Miss Cranstone has suffered a little accident."

Inouyiti writhed in his chair. "She was turned away from the Institute by your servant, Madame Messonier. Why did you not save her, for my sake, Teroni? Why, why——"

"Peace, boy. Beatrice will attend to your lady-love. No harm shall come to Miss Cranstone. Drink a little of this wine. Let us both drink to your lady-love, my dear Soto. Within a week she will be walking in the gardens."

"With Renwick!" the boy groaned. "He is playing the good Samaritan while I am daily represented in a hundred newspapers as an abominable miscreant!"

"All artists are miscreants!" chuckled the nerve specialist. "Am I not an artist? And yet I am merely extracting a little fat from a coterie of overfed poodles."

"Hohenhoff is a handsome fellow," Inouyiti protested. "Somewhat of an athlete and a gentleman. He is going to marry your Beatrice!"

Tsarka stiffened at the unexpected announcement, then shook his head doubtingly.

"We waste time, Inouyiti. Beatrice loves only her profession. No princes for her. She has the world to conquer."

"Hohenhoff will provide her with a little kingdom or principality somewhere on the borders of Saxony. I hope she will not forget that I sent her a husband, Teroni."

The wine moved Soto to mirth in spite of his pain; he sat back laughing immoderately, his white teeth rattling against the wineglass.

"You will be taking a wife yourself if we are smart, Soto. Listen!" Tsarka waited until the fit of mirth had passed, and then continued: "Miss Cranstone is first on the list among those who are to be cured, Inouyiti. Are you listening, boy?"

"My soul is awake, Teroni, although my head is spinning from the effects of your poisonous decoction."

"Well, Miss Cranstone will be treated to-morrow providing we can obtain sufficient radium to conduct the operation. Are you listening, boy with the soul?"

"Horubu has the radium, Teroni. Seek Horubu."

"He came home drunk. The Jew dealers bartered with him for the whole six grains. I want you to induce Paul Isaacson to come here, Soto. I will give you his Hatton Garden address. You have a persuasive manner; use it for Miss Cranstone's sake."

A gentle ringing at the door bell came with startling suddenness upon them. Tsarka slipped into the passage, alert and half-puzzled.

"Who is that?" he demanded, his hand on the lock.

"Your daughter Pepio. Open; it is raining beetles and goblins, and Pepio is very tired."

Tsarka flung wide the door and almost snatched his daughter inside. All his paternal regard evaporated at the thought of the peril induced by her unexpected return.

"Fool . . . destroyer of my fortune! Do you not understand the risks you are running?" he almost shouted when the door was safely closed.

Pepio waved her gloved hand deprecatingly as she placed her fur stole and hat on the hall stand. Her face was unduly flushed, her eyes danced in the electric flare.

"Renwick thought fit to let me go," she explained. "He is more like a young priest than a detective."

"He let you go only to track you here!" her father declared. "Oh, miserable woman, what have you done?"

Tsarka followed her into the study, where Inouyiti sat laughing at his tragic despair.

Pepio made a very pretty salaam to the young artist. "If you are laughing at my father," she said sweetly, "I will teach you better manners."

"You have been with Renwick," the artist retorted, "the man who is going to present us each with twenty years' penal servitude."

"He says that you are related to a beetle, Soto," she answered sweetly, "and that your shooting would shame a horse marine, whatever that may be."

Inouyiti leaped from the chair at the taunt. "Tell your Renwick that when I fired at his baby face my heart cried within me. Tell him I will shoot better next time. There shall be no misses!"

"Peace, peace." Tsarka fretted wolf-like as he paced the study floor, his eyes questing from time to time over Pepio's flushed face. At any moment a posse of plain-clothes police might appear about the house. Renwick, he felt sure, had liberated his daughter with a view to following her in secret.

"You returned in the train?" He leaned across the table, his face thrust out, "and then walked from the station to this house, eh?"

Pepio laughed lightly. "Mr. Renwick promised that he would not follow me after he was assured that Beatrice Messonier would treat Miss Cranstone. He is very interested in Miss Cranstone," she said with a malicious glance at the sullen-browed artist.

Tsarka laughed in spite of himself.

"Renwick knows that a few hours' delay would mean blindness for the pretty comedy actress. He fears to arrest me while her sight is in jeopardy — the fool!"

"A fool, because he has a noble heart!" Pepio cried indignantly. "Did he not suffer the horrors of blindness at the hands of that scoundrel, Horubu! Can you not see something heroic in a man who sacrifices duty and honour to help a struggling artiste?" Pepio's voice had a note of genuine passion.

"It is Gifford Renwick who suffers most, not the Maristers or the Prince Hohenhoffs," she went on. "By a single movement he had our plans from A to Z. Yet he sacrifices fame and promotion in allowing you to go free!"

In her anger she smote Inouyiti's upturned face with her tight-twisted gloves.

"It is Renwick's pity for your lady-love that is our salvation. Once she is out of danger, hide yourself, for he will catch you, Soto, even though you run to the icebergs for shelter!"

Inouyiti quailed under her castigating words. His Japanese pride winced at the thought of the white man's magnanimity.

His misery grew sharper each moment. Violet Cranstone would return to her profession to remember him only as the foreign devil who had almost burnt the light from her eyes with his radium-poisoned stereoscope.

"I will show them what it is to have a soul!" he almost sobbed. "Nothing shall prevail against the genius of Soto Inouyiti. I will paint a picture with my blood, a picture of an artist's crucifixion. I will nail myself to the cross with my own heart and pulse beats."

His long, black hair fell shadow-like over his brow. The trumpet blast of youth sounded in each word. Tsarka glanced up from his deep broodings amazed. Pepio merely laughed.

"Why, you don't know umber from burnt sienna. Didn't the critics say that your technique had spiders in it?"

Inouyiti glared at his pretty tormentor, robbed of speech by her merciless raillery.

Tsarka stopped his ears to escape the jangle of their voices. His thoughts were with Horubu, lying in the dark corner of the laboratory, wounded and seared beyond recovery.

The ex-soldier had paid the penalty of his incurable selfishness and treachery. The strange duel in the laboratory had been fought on equal terms. A trained shot and a skilled fighter, the Manchurian veteran had gone down before the burning contents of the iron ladle.

He was aroused from his thoughts by his daughter's voice.

"Father, I am hungry. Where is the food, the cheese, the bread, and that basket of fruit we ordered yesterday?"

In the midst of their peril Pepio's appetite remained unappeased. Her inspired fingers unearthed pots of preserves and packages of Eastern delicacies with unerring promptitude. Eating French dainties and tormenting Soto Inouyiti were the real pleasures of her existence.

"You two had better marry," Tsarka droned, his eyes on the quarrelling pair.

"Not to a man who intends crucifying himself in an oleograph," Pepio answered, her mouth full of preserved ginger.

"You do not understand," Soto protested. "I meant that my crucified spirit would be revealed in my next work, that was all."

Doctor Tsarka paused in his brief walk up and down the narrow study, and looked fixedly at the young artist.

"You avoid my simple question, my dear Soto.   Why not marry Pepio and go to New York?"

Soto squirmed with Japanese horror.   "I cannot forget Violet.   My heart is ashes. Besides, Pepio does not want me for a husband."

Pepio spread a layer of marmalade over an ice wafer and spoke with it between her white teeth.

"Once upon a time Soto created a spotted baron and a purple-whiskered millionaire. The newspapers now call him the microbe artist from Tokyo."

"It is a lie," Inouyiti screamed.   "The gazettes called it the crime of the century. I am a colossal figure in the public eye, not a microbe, Pepio!"

After Inouyiti had retired for the night and Pepio was locked safely in her room, Doctor Tsarka descended to the laboratory and switched on the electric light.

The furnace fire had burned to a dull red glow, and he stood over it silently, his hands outspread to catch the last rays of warmth. Outside he heard the rain fluting in the spout, the rush of wind in the furnace chimney. He sighed wearily, and then moved nearer the supine figure on the great coat. Stooping, he touched the brown hand pressed against the floor.

"The lion tooth of pain has not yet left you, comrade. What is it that I can do?" he asked tenderly.

Horubu moved and his breath came in laboured gusts.

"A little more fire, Teroni, would have sent me in peace to the Shadows. Only a little more fire. Yes . . . I would like to sleep, comrade. After the fight there should be peace between men. My head is molten. Do you think there is a chance . . . ?"

"No, but you shall sleep well to-night, Horubu, since the gods permit the use of this."

He took from his pocket a small syringe, and then raised the fire-scorched wrist to the light.

Creeping to Inouyiti's room, an hour later, Tsarka shook the sleeping boy gently.

"The idea has come at last, Soto," he

whispered. "Men who handle radium constantly become possessed of two devils — one good, one full of malice toward human kind."

Soto rubbed his eyes. "There is no doubt about the one that inhabits Teroni Tsarka," he said drowsily. "It has a pair of pink eyes and a fiery tail. I shall paint it for a pantomime book."

Doctor Tsarka sat beside his bed scarce able to restrain the laughter that rose in him. "I have an idea, Soto, that Renwick is the only man who can harm us. We cannot kill him, but he can be arrested!"

Soto sat up in the bed, his long, black hair thrust back from his forehead.

"Renwick is a detective. The English do not arrest their own officials!" he gasped.

"When they are dishonest, Soto, it is possible to get them into prison. This Gifford accepted a cheque for two hundred guineas from Pepio, some time ago. It bore my signature. The bank still has it, although my account has long been withdrawn. To-night I shall get Kotio Maru to inform Scotland Yard that Renwick is the prime mover in the studio outrage. Kotio knows English

law. He will make it clear that Renwick
took our money. They will call it complicity
— aiding and abetting us, the people who
engineered the Whitehall Motor Atrocity
and the Piccadilly Studio Outrage; eh, my
Soto."

"It will not help us!" Inouyiti declared.
"Renwick will tell everything to Scotland
Yard. Instead of eluding one man we shall
have a dozen on our heels. Tsarka . . .
you are mad?"

Inouyiti lay back on the pillow, waving
off, with both hands, the man who sought to
disturb his dreams of fame.

"Renwick will not put Scotland Yard
on our heels," Tsarka insisted. "Do you
think he has worked and suffered so silently
only to blab the result of his hard-won
investigations to his rivals in the chase?
I am not mad, Inouyiti. Only a little care
and wisdom are needed to keep Renwick under
lock and key until we have annexed the
Marister fee and the Hohenhoff guineas.
Scotland Yard will then wake up and find us
gone."

CHAPTER XVII

GIFFORD was like a man swimming in an octopus-infested lagoon. At any moment an unseen tentacle might drag him to the bottom. He had given Pepio a chance on the definite understanding that Miss Cranstone should receive instant treatment at the Radium Institute, a circumstance not likely to commend itself to his employer.

During the days that followed his meeting with the Japanese girl he moved about the City as one who had committed himself to an undesirable compact. His solicitude for Miss Cranstone had caused him to waver slightly from the strict path of duty, he told himself. He was determined, however, to continue his investigations and end the little reign of terror resulting from the radium gang's operations in the City.

He turned, one morning, in the direction of the Messonier Institute with a definite course of action shaped in his mind. Ar-

riving at the portals he proffered his card to
the hall attendant, and was conducted into
a green-panelled consulting room to await the
coming of Beatrice Messonier.

She came in in a mauve-hued gown that
somehow recalled the deadly colour-flashes
he had experienced during the weeks of his
radium blindness. She greeted him coldly,
and he detected a veiled hostility in her manner
which puzzled him not a little.

"You have come to inquire after Miss
Cranstone," she said with professional
brevity.

He bowed. "It is of your colleague, Doctor
Tsarka, I wish to speak."

She smiled faintly. "After our conversation the other day, Mr. Renwick, I have
no doubt what you have in your mind. Pray
proceed."

"I came here to warn you," he continued,
"that it will now be my business to insure
Doctor Tsarka's arrest!"

"Then why come to me?" she flashed back.
"Is it customary for private detectives to
notify the friends of the person they are
about to surrender to the police?"

"Not always, madame. In the present

instance I feel that I could not act without your confidence."

She laughed a trifle bitterly. "Please proceed, Mr. Renwick. You are very kind."

"I am kind enough to remember that you once saved my reason, Madame Messonier," he went on. "I consider that Doctor Tsarka is your friend, therefore I warn you that his capture by the police may be effected at any moment."

His words seemed to shatter her self-restraint. She faced him with a flame-spot on her cheek.

"You must not arrest Doctor Tsarka. You know that he is not guilty of the studio crime!"

Gifford glanced at her in mild astonishment. "Teroni Tsarka is a pronounced criminal. I fell into his hands upon one occasion, and it was you who saved me from the effects of his radium sponge."

"Doctor Tsarka declared that it was an accident," she retorted. "You had no legal right in his laboratory!"

Silence fell between them, a silence in which the woman could hear the beating of her own heart. She was first to speak.

"I want you to spare Doctor Tsarka," she half pleaded. "Have I your promise?"

"I cannot promise to shield him, Madame Messonier. War has been declared between us!"

"Oh!" She regarded him now in half-amused wonderment. "Pray, Mr. Renwick, spare me, I beg you, when your operations come to a close."

"What do you mean, madame?" He approached her by half a step as though to read in her eyes the veiled satire of her words.

She laughed outright. "I am merely amused at your want of discretion, Mr. Renwick. You came to me a few days ago begging for the light in Violet Cranstone's eyes. Doctor Tsarka instructed me to proceed with the operation instantly. Was there any criminal motive in that?"

Gifford was silent.

She regarded him steadily.

"Now that you imagine Miss Cranstone to be in a fair way of recovery, you begin to shadow this Institute in the hope of catching my old associate."

"It is only a question of days," he said wearily, "before the Japanese gang is broken up."

"There is no gang, Mr. Renwick. It only exists in your imagination. Doctor Tsarka has been the victim of circumstances. He is a generous, noble-hearted man who has spent half his life in ministering to afflicted humanity. In the bitterest days of my early career he assisted me without a hope of compensation."

"But . . . Inouyiti and Horubu are his friends," Gifford protested. "Please remember, Madame Messonier, that Soto is responsible for the studio crime."

She smiled compassionately at the young detective. "Soto Inouyiti is insane. No one but a lunatic would have conceived such a tragic farce. The boy is under medical surveillance, has been for months past. His friends never suspected that he would organize so dastardly an outrage!"

Gifford sighed, and was about to withdraw. "I must wish you good morning, madame," he said suavely. "I regret that I do not share your opinion of Doctor Tsarka."

"Then you will give the signal for his arrest?" She followed to the door of the Institute, and for the first time Gifford detected something of the pantheress in her stride.

"Positively," he answered looking back. "It is my duty."

He paused again to stare into the gray depths of her eyes. It was as though naked steel had flashed between them. The transformation in her was electrical. White to the lips, and with fingers clenched, she spoke with her firm round chin thrust out.

"Do you know that Miss Cranstone is at this moment in my operating theatre?"

"No; I was not aware of the fact."

"Well, she does not return to her home until to-morrow. I deemed it advisable for her to remain here."

"But . . . she is out of danger!"

"In so short a period, Mr. Renwick? I am not a miracle-worker. I do not restore the blind with a touch of my hand."

He met her glance unwaveringly. "You will restore Miss Cranstone," he predicted. "Nothing is more certain."

"Love is so full of faith," she laughed ironically. "It is proof against even the terrors of darkness."

Something in her words struck cold as death upon him. "Does the physician doubt her powers?" he asked with a sick taste in his mouth. He could not reconcile the clenched hand with the smile on her lips.

"One never knows how deeply the radium fire has burnt," she vouchsafed with professional promptitude. "Until to-day I considered Doctor Tsarka my good genius. In my moments of doubt I rely on his excellent recommendations. Now you threaten to take him from me. Good-by, Mr. Renwick."

She was gone, and he found himself staring bleakly into the crowded thoroughfare adjoining the Institute.

Behind madame's silken courtesy he detected the claw of the tigress. Her meaning was quite clear. She had tactically defied him to arrest her patron, Doctor Tsarka. With Violet Cranstone in her keeping she could compel his obedience. Yet his anger did not rise against Beatrice Messonier. She firmly believed in Tsarka's innocence, and would probably use every known means in her power to shield him.

A cab took him to Mrs. Cranstone's house. He was admitted without a moment's delay. The mother of the young comedy actress met him with outstretched hands.

"How delighted I am to see you, Mr.

Renwick!" she exclaimed with genuine fervour. "Nothing that we can do will ever repay the priceless service you have rendered us."

Mrs. Cranstone's face expressed the new hope which had come since Violet had been admitted to the Radium Institute.

Gifford's tense, drawn manner relaxed under her smiling welcome. "I understood that Miss Cranstone was to become an outdoor patient," he said after a while. "Did she enter the Institute voluntarily?"

"No; madame sent for her quite unexpectedly. Her request that my daughter should undergo uninterrupted treatment alarmed me at first. Until the crisis was over it was imperative, she said, that Violet should remain at the Institute. Of course, there was no alternative but to comply with madame's wishes."

Mrs. Cranstone brightened perceptibly as she concluded her statement. "Between ourselves, Mr. Renwick, I am of opinion that madame has conceived quite a sisterly regard for my daughter," she added with a motherly glow of pride.

Gifford talked to gain a moment's respite

from Mrs. Cranstone's overflowing exuberance. He was certain that Beatrice Messonier had visited Tsarka within the last few days, and that the little nerve specialist had moved her to pity and compassion for his dire extremity. Beatrice had gained possession of Violet with the idea of using her as a weapon against him. He could not confide his terrible suspicions to Mrs. Cranstone, for he knew that any statement of his would only serve to aggravate the situation.

He took his leave after promising to call again during the week. In the street he asked himself the question which dominated every other issue in his mind. Would Beatrice Messonier dare to delay Miss Cranstone's recovery until Tsarka had made good his escape? How far would this incomparable lady physician go in her efforts to save the man she venerated and to whom she owed a debt of everlasting gratitude?

Gifford fought with himself for a solution of the terrible problem that now presented itself. To arrest Tsarka would be to signal for Beatrice to work some evil upon Violet Cranstone. One touch from her hand would plunge the young lady into outer darkness

forever.   And who was to judge Beatrice
Messonier, he asked himself. A woman
skilled in the use of the most mysterious of
modern curative elements! The merest pressure of her finger at the wrong moment would
place Violet Cranstone beyond all chance of
recovery.

He told himself, with a heart that could
not breathe, that Violet Cranstone's misfortune had not swung him from his ordinary
path of duty.   He was not anxious to commit
what seemed to him the everlasting sin of
murder, for he knew well enough that Violet's
whole future lay in his decision to forego
hostilities against the Japanese doctor.

In the City he encountered Tony Hackett
for the first time since the studio outrage.
Gifford, without hesitation, explained everything which had happened since their last
meeting. Hackett, whose half-hearted operations against the Japs had ended through lack
of information, listened pensively to his
young friend's confidences. His slightly
bored expression changed gradually to one
of amazement at the conclusion of Renwick's
narrative.

"When Pepio was in your hands, why

didn't you nab her father?" he broke out.
"You had the game on the table. Oh, Gif,
what a bungle you've made of it!'

Gifford lit a cigarette dejectedly, while the
roar of the City's traffic came upon him with
the sound of waves beating on a sandy key.
He heard the rush and sob of motors, the
querulous shouts of the newsboys, and through
it all he could almost see the figure of Beatrice
Messonier peering through her retinoscope
into the radium-tortured eyes of Violet Cranstone. Then he turned, almost sharply, to
his old comrade.

"If we got Tsarka arrested the Radium
Institute would close with a snap, Tony."

"Well, how does that affect Mr. Gifford
Renwick?" Tony demanded cheerfully.

"It would affect the lives of three innocent
people," the young detective answered. "I've
never smiled in the face of a tigress," he
added grimly, "but to-day I saw a live
pantheress in the eyes of a certain lady
physician!"

"A bit of professional bluff, my dear boy.
She won't dare maltreat Miss Cranstone."

Gifford passed a restless night. The shadow
of the Radium Institute loomed Titanesque

through his dreams. If by chance some member of Scotland Yard arrested Teroni Tsarki the consequences would be hard to foresee.

He found himself the following morning pacing the eastern side of the Institute, his glance wandering at times to the high, square windows of the operating theatre where he had spent so many hours while undergoing treatment.

He could not shake from his mind a conviction that Miss Cranstone's case was being unnecessarily delayed. His nerves leaped at the possibility of her needless pain and suffering. It was now eleven o'clock, the hour chosen by Beatrice for her morning operations, and he knew that in all probability Violet was at that very moment seated in the chair of torture.

Up and down he paced, the dull boom of the traffic in his ears. Turning the street angle slowly he walked past the white doors of the Institute, pausing an instant to glance inside.

The sound of hurrying feet on the stairs attracted him; a white-capped nurse fled down the wide hall, calling as she ran to the liveried attendant standing in one of the numerous recesses.

The attendant emerged, his face betraying instant trepidation and alarm. He called after the vanishing nurse in a slightly high-pitched voice:

"Which doctor did you say, miss? I didn't quite hear what you said."

The nurse's white cap flashed into view again.

"Doctor Tsarka!" she exclaimed hurriedly. "Ring him up. There has been a terrible accident in the operating room. Oh, dear, do make haste!"

The attendant appeared unable to comprehend the meaning of her words. He remained staring incredulously about him until Gifford sprang up the steps to his side.

"Get madame's telephone book and look up Doctor Tsarka's address!" he commanded. "You understand that there has been an accident."

The nurse turned in surprise upon the young detective. Then her manner softened instantly; for she recognized him as one of madame's earlier patients.

"Thank you, Mr. Renwick," she said as

he gripped the telephone receiver and waited for the attendant to read Tsarka's private address. It came from an unexpected quarter. A voice on the stairs gave it out sharply, "Five, six, three, eight, Purfew-on-Thames."

Gifford caught his breath sharply as he repeated the number to the central exchange.

A few seconds later the unmistakable voice of Doctor Tsarka sounded in his ear.

"Well?"

"The Messonier Institute," Gifford answered. "Something serious has happened in Madame Messonier's operating room. Madame begs you to come to her assistance."

Gifford waited, half in dread, for the little nerve specialist's reply. A fear entered him suddenly that Tsarka had recognized his voice. The answer soothed his alarms.

"Tell madame that I am coming as fast as my Panhard will allow."

Gifford turned to the nurse as she sped past with a blue-labelled jar in her hand.

"One moment, Miss Dixon," he began hurriedly. "Can you tell me exactly what has happened, so that I may be of further service to Madame Messonier?"

The nurse halted on the stairs, her blanched cheeks and unsteady gait hinting at some terror over which she had no control.

"Is it Miss Cranstone who has . . . met with the accident?" He was like a man standing at the grave of his last hope.

"I am not certain," the nurse answered hurriedly. "Madame was operating on Miss Cranstone, and the Butoni glass coil exploded, striking madame in the face."

"Then Miss Cranstone is not hurt?"

"I cannot say. The glass coil contained something very peculiar. It burst in all directions. I can't really say how far it has affected Miss Cranstone."

The nurse hurried away, leaving him a prey to his own dread imaginings. He could not force an entrance into the operating theatre, or even attempt an investigation. Anything might have happened, he told himself. Yet he dared not believe Beatrice Messonier capable of a surgical crime. A radium tube had burst and he must wait, with a show of patience, until the arrival of Teroni Tsarka.

CHAPTER XVIII

A FEW minutes later the nurse appeared at the stair-head calling him softly by name.

"Oh, please come up, madame will be glad of your presence."

Gifford mounted the stairs willingly, and followed the nurse down the long corridor to the green doors of the operating room.

He was conscious of a dazzling white light as he stepped inside. His eye was caught instantly by a pair of disc mirrors suspended over the operating chair in the centre of the room. Beatrice Messonier was seated on a couch.

It was evident to him that she was suffering acutely. Her left hand pressed a wet handkerchief over her eyes, from which arose the odour of an unknown chemical preparation. She appeared conscious of his presence, and addressed him without raising her head.

"I have experienced a slight accident with

one of my tubes, Mr. Renwick. Nurse Dixon informed me of your presence."

Gifford expressed instant sympathy, while his glance wandered across the operating room for some sign of Miss Cranstone. There was none.

Madame appeared to guess the trend of his thoughts. "Miss Cranstone has retired to her room," she explained, the 'kerchief still pressed to her eyes. "It was unfortunate that she was in the operating chair at the moment of the accident. I have sent for Doctor Tsarka, to ——"

She paused to tighten the 'kerchief as though the pain was more than she could bear.

"To attend Miss Cranstone?" he hazarded.

"No, no; I shall require his services myself."

"Is he the nearest specialist, madame?"

"The nearest is often the farthest, Mr. Renwick. Doctor Tsarka will know exactly what has happened. By his aid I shall be able to neutralize the effects of the bursting bulb. Any other physician would only bother me and probably endanger my sight."

She sat up with difficulty, her breath coming in sharp expulsions.

"Are you determined to carry out your threat against Doctor Tsarka?" she demanded with unexpected suddenness.

"Will you allow me to see Miss Cranstone before I answer your question, Madame Messonier? You were operating on her at the time of the accident."

Beatrice Messonier seemed to be holding herself from an outburst of indignation.

"I know what is in your mind. You think me capable of the most dastardly of surgical crimes, Mr. Renwick!"

Gifford paled. "I have only your welfare at heart, Madame Messonier. The other day you hinted at the possibility of delay in Miss Cranstone's cure if Tsarka were arrested. Of course, I misconstrued your real meaning."

"Will you allow him to come here and attend me?"

"I shall not prevent him attending your injuries, Madame Messonier."

"Thank you, Mr. Renwick. Now will you kindly touch the bell near the door. I want to prove that I am not a scientific barbarian."

The nurse appeared and, at a nod from Beatrice Messonier, passed swiftly along the passage, leaving Gifford to guess the cause of her errand.

It seemed an eternity before the soft swishing of a skirt broke the intolerable silence. The nurse opened the door gently to allow Violet Cranstone to enter. Gifford looked up in speechless wonderment. The face of the young comedy actress had undergone an amazing beatification. The dark eyes which had flinched from the light of an ordinary lamp were now illumined by the tender flashes of youth. She stared inquiringly at Beatrice and then at the boyish figure of Gifford Renwick.

Madame divined the cause of their embarrassment. Even in her pain she could not repress a smile.

"You ought to know Mr. Renwick," she said to her young patient. "Since the terrible studio accident he has presided like a guardian angel over your affairs."

The young comedy actress took Gifford's hand with a cry of genuine delight. The terror of the shade had vanished forever. She was free to return to her home with the joy of life and the pulse of ambition beating within her.

"Only for your help, Mr. Renwick, I should have become a human derelict indeed; for it was you who urged the Messonier cure in the face of my mother's opposition."

There was no mistaking the natural health and spirits which bubbled within Violet Cranstone. Gifford felt how unjust had been his fears concerning Beatrice's intentions.

The radium specialist broke in upon his thoughts unexpectedly.

"Miss Cranstone returns to her home this evening — cured, as you see. Will you stay here until she is quite ready to go?"

Gifford expressed himself delighted. His short eulogy on Miss Cranstone's wonderful recovery was cut short by a light footfall in the passage outside. The door was pushed open. Doctor Tsarka, dressed in heavy motor clothes, entered unannounced. His face was pinched and haggard, his lips tight drawn. A dark flush crossed him at sight of the young detective.

"I was not aware that you had invited this young gentleman to meet me, Beatrice," he said with biting emphasis.

"Mr. Renwick has declared an amnesty, my dear doctor. He has been good enough to allow you to come here and render aid to your old pupil." There was a touch of bitterness in her words that did not escape Gifford. He merely bowed, however, in response to Tsarka's acidulous greeting.

"I trust that Madame Messonier will soon be out of pain, Doctor Tsarka. Your skill and knowledge should not leave her case in doubt for one moment."

The Jap doctor had thrown aside his motor-coat, his professional instincts agog at sight of Beatrice's pain and distress. Such a personage as Gifford Renwick did not exist from the moment his old pupil arranged herself in the operating chair.

The young detective could only admire the silken ease and delicacy with which Tsarka conducted his examination. Then, becoming aware of the urgency for instant silence, he led Miss Cranstone to an inner room which was part of the operating chamber. Here he was determined to wait until Tsarka had pronounced upon the effects of the bursting bulb.

Miss Cranstone was like one newly released

from a dark cell. The sight of a huge bowl of flowers in the window recess filled her with ecstasy. The terror of blindness was gone at last. Never more would she experience the javelin-like shafts of pain which had threatened to blind her. She turned to Gifford, and her face grew inexpressibly tender as she spoke.

"One day, when the light faded and left me groping from chair to chair, I touched a rose that some one had placed near me. The perfume was there, but somehow it felt black to the touch. Did you experience that feeling during your radium blindness?"

"Yes; the radium shut out my little world, too," he answered gently. "It cast a blot over the sky and the fields. I saw things through a violet shroud at first, and, finally, nothing at all until Messonier rent the shroud and permitted the light to pour in."

They sat in silence for a while, breathing like two children who had met each other in some vague dreamland from which they had only just emerged.

The face of Doctor Tsarka peering in at the door shattered the blissful reverie which promised to engulf them.

"Mr. Renwick," he said sharply. "there are two Scotland Yard men coming up the stairs. Is this how you keep your amnesty?" he cried with rising anger.

Gifford muttered a word of apology to Miss Cranstone, and joined the Jap doctor in the doorway.

"I am not responsible for their visit," he declared warmly. "I will keep them out of the operating room since you desire it."

Quick as thought he closed and locked the green doors that overlooked the entrance hall below just as the two figures reached the stair-head. Turning to Tsarka he spoke again in a scarce audible voice.

"Pray continue your work, sir. We shall find a means of maintaining our amnesty," he added grimly.

Tsarka saluted with military precision, and then silently returned to his patient in the operating chair.

A growing admiration for the little Jap's nerve and coolness came upon Gifford as he joined Miss Cranstone. The young actress was turning the pages of an album carelessly. She looked up at the sound of his footsteps.

"Do you think that madame is seriously

hurt, Mr. Renwick? I was present when the tube burst, and for a while her face was enveloped in a voilet mist. I hope her sight is not affected."

"Doctor Tsarka is capable. of surgical miracles where radium is concerned," Gifford answered gravely. "At present he is likely to be interrupted."

A loud knocking at the door outside verified Gifford's statement. Violet Cranstone glanced up inquiringly. Gifford spoke without a lift in his voice.

"The men outside are detectives. They have come to effect Tsarka's arrest. Would it be right for me to let them in?"

He heard her quick breathing, and knew instinctively that his words had struck at the roots of her moral fibre. She had drawn away slightly as though suddenly afraid.

"Is — is Doctor Tsarka a criminal?" Her lips were dry, ashen.

"Yes, in my estimation, Miss Cranstone."

"Why do you put such a question to me?"

"Because I am losing my sense of moral responsibility." He looked up now and met her swift glance. The banging at the door grew more violent. A rough, authoritative voice called upon Beatrice Messonier to open without further delay.

Gifford continued as though nothing unusual, were happening. "I would like your advice in this matter, Miss Cranstone," he went on. "Assuming that Tsarka is a criminal, would you hold me guilty for attempting to shield him in the present instance?"

"Will those detectives take him away?"

"Yes."

"And Beatrice Messonier? What will become of her and the people depending for their lives on her aid?"

Gifford was silent. The loud voices of the men outside became more distinct, but to the little Jap doctor they were apparently non-existent. Bending over the chair, he proceeded with his examination as though the two officers of the law were dream phantoms.

Violet Cranstone touched Gifford's bent shoulder very gently.

"You will not let them arrest Doctor Tsarka? What wrong has he committed?"

"The studio affair was the result of his machinations. Were you not a victim? Have you no desire to see him punished?"

Violet's lips tightened perceptibly. "I have no right to judge him. I only desire to see Beatrice Messonier freed from her present agony."

Gifford walked to the door of the operating room and spoke to the men outside.

"What do you want?" he demanded firmly.

An instant's pause followed his question. Then one of the detectives spoke in unusually gruff tones.

" I have a warrant for the arrest of Gifford Renwick," he said. "He is in this building . . . Are you Renwick?"

"Yes; and the charge?" Gifford began to resent what he fancied to be an impudent attempt at practical joking. "You know that I am an International man," he added curtly.

"Very sorry, Mr. Renwick," was the sharp reply. "I'll read the charge when you open the door. We're acting on information laid — that cheque for two hundred guineas you accepted from the Jap radium clique."

"The Tsarka cheque!" Gifford's mind reeled back to the two hundred guineas which Pepio had given him to cover Beatrice

Messonier's fee when the radium blindness was on him.

"Who's charging me with — with ——"

"For being concerned with the Tsarka gang?" the voice prompted. "Oh, we were advised of the business by a Japanese named Kotio Maru. You know him, of course?"

"Never heard of him," Gifford declared vehemently.

The two detectives outside appeared to relish the business of arresting one of Anthony Coleman's men. Their laughter fell jarringly on Renwick's ears. Glancing over his shoulder he saw that the Jap doctor was watching him attentively.

"You will not open that door, Mr. Renwick," he said sharply. "I am not ready."

Gifford nodded approval, and again addressed the two Scotland Yard men.

"I must ask you to wait a little while, gentlemen. If you will go downstairs I will join you in the consulting room."

The two detectives whispered together and then descended the stairs slowly. Simultaneously the Jap doctor assisted Beatrice from the chair, bowing to Renwick as he did so.

"Madame is not seriously hurt," he confided. "To-morrow she will be much better.
I must go now."

"Not downstairs, or by the front entrance,"
Gifford warned. "There are probably a
couple of men posted outside the Institute."

"There is a secret exit at the rear."

"You will save yourself trouble by remaining here, Doctor Tsarka. The moment I
surrender myself those officials downstairs
will go with me."

Beatrice suppressed a little scream. "Do
you mean that you are to be arrested?" she
cried. "For what reason?"

Gifford consulted his watch thoughtfully.
"For accepting a cheque from Pepio Tsarka,"
he said stonily.

Beatrice turned to her old *confrère* inquiringly. "Do you know how the cheque
came into the possession of the police, my
dear Doctor?"

Tsarka shrugged with an affectation of
weariness. "I knew nothing of the cheque
until Pepio had given it to Mr. Renwick.
She is a very impulsive child. I gave it to her
to pay some of her bills in the City. It is
very unfortunate."

Violet Cranstone stole forward, a listening fear in her eyes. Gifford laughed lightly, but behind his unassailable composure lay the knowledge of failure and ruin.

Violet Cranstone stood beside him as a comrade clings to a stricken friend.

"I am so sorry, Mr. Renwick. Surely there is some terrible mistake?"

Gifford remembered afterward the pain in her eyes, the memory of which helped to sweeten the bitterest hours of his life. In the present instance his thoughts were for the Japanese doctor's safety. He had given his assurance that no harm should befall the operating specialist.

"You had better stay here until I am gone," he said to Tsarka.

Without a word the Jap doctor slipped into a side room and locked the door. Gifford held out his hand to Beatrice Messonier.

"Good-by, madame. If any unjust suspicions entered me concerning your professional integrity, I ask your pardon — humbly."

He opened the door swiftly, but his movements were not swift enough to prevent Violet Cranstone joining him. Their bond of friendship was not to be easily set aside.

"I am going, too," she declared vehemently. "What sin have you committed that you should be dragged to prison?"

Gifford assured her blithely that he possessed friends in high places who would not permit of any injustice befalling him. Violet came very near to crying aloud as he touched her hand with his lips. Then, without a word, he walked briskly down the wide stairs and surrendered himself to the officers of the law.

CHAPTER XIX

THE news of Gifford's arrest on a charge of accepting money and being concerned with the notorious Tsarka gang cast a shadow of gloom over the International Inquiry Bureau. The fact that Gifford had taken the cheque at a time when blindness assailed him would not lessen the offence in the eyes of a jury, his friends predicted.

"Men who temporize with Japanese criminals must beware of their strangling fingers. I would sooner play hide and seek with a tiger than expose my reputation to the mercies of these radium swindlers."

Tony Hackett sat back in his cubicle at the International Bureau and smoked thoughtfully. His chief had peeped in for a moment to exchange views on the unexpected development in the Tsarka operations, and had retired with Tony's words ringing in his ears.

Tony's thoughts circled around the whirlpool of incidents which had led to his friend's arrest. Some one had sacrificed Gifford with the intention of removing him permanently from the service. His detention, on a charge of complicity, would allow the Tsarka gang a clear field, for Tony knew that Gifford Renwick was the only man in England who had divined the subtle workings of Tsarka's organization.

Touching a bell at his elbow, he waited until a small hook-nosed man peeped in at the door. Hackett beckoned with his forefinger.

"Come in, Carr, and please don't peep round the door like a debt collector."

Carr entered the room with an affected sprightliness of manner that was lost on the brooding detective.

"Lor' bless you, sir, my peeping round doors comes from sheer habit. There are times, as you know, Mr. Hackett, when the tip of one's nose can do good service."

He took his seat opposite Tony, his thin, nerveless hands clasped on both knees. The detective surveyed him with a benign air.

"Now, Carr, this office regards you as the ablest wire-tapper in the British Isles. You are supposed to know the main arteries of

London's telephone service better than the head operators at the central exchange."

"Thank you, sir." Carr moved in the chair, his eyes questing over Tony's brooding features. "I think I know my business pretty well, Mr. Hackett."

Tony reached down a red-backed book from a shelf and pushed it across the table.

"Look up the Messonier Institute, Carr, and get in touch with their connection early to-morrow. There will be some talking between Madame Messonier and a Japanese doctor. Get his number if possible, and report anything they say."

Carr shuffled his feet uneasily. "It's a risky business, Mr. Hackett, and one that Mr. Coleman strictly forbids, unless it's a matter of life and death."

Hackett pushed a cigar across the table. "I believe you are getting nervous, Carr," he said deliberately. "You know that I am on the track of those Japanese radium swindlers. I've been hitching up my clues since Renwick fell out of line, and I want your help badly."

Carr sighed as the cigar smoke lifted above his head. "Very sorry to hear of Mr. Renwick's trouble, sir. He was always kind to me when things were not so bright as they are now."

"He was foolishly kind to a lot of people," Tony declared. "Kindness and consideration for other people's feelings have landed him where he is."

"A woman in the case you think, sir."

"Four," Tony answered; "but I can't say which one has pulled him off the path of duty. There's a Duchess, a comedy actress, a medical specialist, while the fourth is a dangerously pretty Japanese girl with sloe black eyes."

"It wouldn't be the Duchess, sir," Carr ventured obsequiously. "They never fall in love with private detectives. I'd put my wages on the actress though, if it came to a guessing competiton."

Tony looked up in surprise. "Well, Gif is just the kind of ass to blight his prospects over a girl who has never seen him, and who, in all probability, won't remember him when he comes out of gaol."

Carr rose and sighed as though the news of Renwick's ill-fortune depressed him. Hackett nodded briefly.

"Send me Tsarka's address; the old scoundrel is using a telephone. I'll put an end
to this Gilbertian warfare. Good night,
Carr!"

Now that Gifford had been drawn from the
case Tony felt that he might trap the volatile
band of Japanese swindlers with a fairly clear
conscience.

Early the following morning he returned
to the office to await the result of the professional wire-tapper's investigations. It was
not long in coming.

The first call came at eleven o'clock.
Carr's voice was clearly audible in the receiver as he detailed his morning's experiences.

"Are you listening, Mr. Hackett?"

"Yes, yes; fire away. It's a matter of
life and death to the Bureau, Carr."

"Well, the Duchess of Marister has just
paid in a cheque for five thousand guineas
to Madame Messonier. Doctor Tsarka inquired ten minutes ago."

"Oh! And his address?"

"Twenty-four Abingdon Walk, Purfew-
on-Thames."

"Good!" Tony was about to hang up the
receiver. But Carr had not finished.

"Doctor Tsarka has begged madame to send the money to his house to-day."

Five minutes later Tony was seated with his chief arranging for the simultaneous arrest of Madame Messonier and Teroni Tsarka. Anthony Coleman appeared slightly agitated at the suddenness of Tony's operations.

"Prudence, Hackett, prudence! We must not leave ourselves open to legal action. Madame Messonier is probably a tool of Tsarka. For heaven's sake be cautious."

The little detective grinned amiably. "Well, sir, we'll submit our case to Scotland Yard, and providing they're not eaten up with envy, I'll go with their men and identify Tsarka and that little devil Inouyiti. Our fellows will look after the radium lady's movements."

Hackett's intentions were clear enough now that the telephone-tapper had supplied him with Tsarka's address. Cunning and subterfuge would no longer keep the Japanese swindlers out of gaol. Once in the dock Tony hoped that Tsarka's evidence might release Gifford from his dilemma.

A few hours later, in company with three picked men from Scotland Yard, he journeyed to Purfew, and lost not an instant in gaining Abingdon Walk. Here he quickly posted his assistants in a position to intercept Tsarka or his friends if they attempted to leave or enter the house.

Tony's first move had been to notify the Duchess of Marister concerning the cheque she had passed to Madame Messonier. Would she, in her own interests, cause payment to be stopped until madame's innocence of all complicity with Tsarka had been proved beyond doubt.

The Duchess of Marister's reply to his message was somewhat disappointing. She refused absolutely to cancel payment of her fee. Madame Messonier had performed the most wonderful operation in the world, she declared, had relieved her, in a few short days, of unspeakable pain and torture. Furthermore, Her Grace added that she regarded Beatrice as a twentieth century genius, who had suffered the bitterest humiliation at the hands of the British medical profession.

Tony suppressed his growing anger.

"A bit of feminine affection combined with feminine logic. We'll save the cheque though.

It would only help those Japanese devils to fight us to the bitter end."

"Five thousand guineas will buy them the best legal assistance in England," one of the men hazarded from his coign of vantage near a deserted coal depôt.

The house stood well back from the road; the rear entrance was sheltered by a seven-foot wall, having a gate at the end which Tony soon discovered was securely locked and bolted.

"Grab anything with a Japanese face that tries to enter or comes out," he advised his watching assistants.

Tony was alive to the importance of his operations. The arrest of the Japanese radium clique would be the greatest *coup* of the year. His heart beat a trifle quicker at the possibility of the Duchess's cheque slipping into the hands of Teroni Tsarka.

An hour passed without a sign from the house, and the men fidgeted uneasily at their posts. Why not rush the place? they argued. What was to be gained by waiting outside?

Hackett maintained a Napoleonic silence. He was confident that Madame Messonier's cheque-bearer would arrive before dark. The

question that disturbed him was whether the
messenger would be a man or a woman.

Occasionally a tradesman sauntered past
bearing baskets of foodstuffs and groceries
by way of the side-entrance. A signal from
one of the men turned Hackett's attention to
a red car that flashed, almost without sound,
into the street. It stopped about fifty paces
from Tony's point of observation, and he
saw at a glance that the car carried two chauffeurs, one of whom appeared to be searching
for a particular house number.

The car slid past and halted outside Tsarka's residence. A moment later a tall military man stepped to the pavement, and with
a nod to the chauffeurs, passed through the
house gate.

Tony almost leaped from his hiding place,
his pocket binoculars scrutinizing the two
German eagles embossed on the red panel
of the car.

"Prince Hohenhoff, by Jove!" he gasped.
"Now what in thunder does it mean!"

For a fraction of time the little detective
paused irresolutely before committing himself. Then, casting aside prudence and reserve, rushed forward in time to prevent

the royal visitor from touching the electric bell.

"I must ask your pardon, Prince Hohenhoff," he began breathlessly. "But it is my duty to remind you that this house is under police surveillance!"

Prince Hohenhoff turned, and the little detective beheld two tiny silver scars on his eyelids which recalled the deadly radium burns which had once marred Gifford's features. The Prince was a splendid type of the modern German military school; handsome of feature, and limber as a professional athlete since his recovery. He looked quickly at Tony, and his mouth twitched.

"I am aware that this house is under police surveillance," he responded sharply. "It was for that reason Madame Beatrice Messonier begged me to execute one little favour."

He spoke with a strong native accent, and at each word his eyes seemed to blossom with the fires of passion. Tony was at his wit's end. He knew that the royal visitor was in no way implicated in the big radium swindle; but he guessed in a flash that Beatrice had used him as a messenger to carry the Duchess of Marister's cheque to Tsarka. He could not understand how a mere lady physician had prevailed upon so distinguished a personage to act as her envoy. Tony's lips grew dry.

"I must venture to warn your Royal Highness that you are moving in dangerous society. This house," he indicated the square fronted building briefly, "is the home of a gang of notorious Japanese criminals."

The Prince viewed him in amazement. He stood six inches over Hackett, and his voice had the baying challenge of a Moltke or a Bismarck.

"I regard you as an insolent meddler!" he thundered. "How dare you assume that Madame Messonier is capable of associating with criminals! Gott! you do not know what you are talking about!"

Tony writhed under his glance and stammered an incoherent apology. Yet not for an instant did he budge from the Prince's side.

"I have orders to watch this house," he stated with gathering assurance. "And your Highness' presence here places me and other officials in a curious position."

Hackett's protest was cut short by the

abrupt opening of the house door. The face
of Horubu's servant appeared. He smiled
obsequiously at both men, and waited with
lowered head for some indication of their
business.

The Prince addressed him in English.
"Tell Doctor Tsarka that I have come from
Madame Messonier." He drew an envelope
from his pocket, holding it firmly between
finger and thumb. "This gentleman," he
indicated Tony with an unmistakable air of
suspicion, "has made a very grave statement
in regard to your master."

Satuma beamed and fell into a salaaming
attitude, but not for an instant did his eyes
leave the envelope in the Prince's hand. He
thrust out his long brown fingers as though to
take it, but discovered that the hand of a
German prince is sometimes as swift as a
conjuror's. The envelope was withdrawn
sharply.

"If your master will do me the honour,"
he laughed, "I will hand the letter to him
personally. "It is part of a promise I made
to Madame Messonier."

Tony held himself like one about to plunge
from a height. "I trust your Highness will

allow me to be present at the interview.   That envelope" — he pointed to the letter in Hohenhoff's hand — "contains a cheque from the Duchess of Marister for five thousand guineas. It is my duty to safeguard her interests."

Prince Hohenhoff eyed the little detective shrewdly, while the coolie servant withdrew to carry the royal visitor's message to the waiting Japanese doctor.

Again Tony asked himself how a Prince of a reigning house could have been induced to join in one of the most transparent frauds of the century.   It was evident that Beatrice had utilized her genius to some purpose.   A glance at Hohenhoff's handsome face proved that her science and skill had completely overtaken the terrible effects of the radium poisoning.   Like most newly convalescent patients, the Prince had proved sufficiently malleable, Tony thought, to conform to his fair physician's slightest wish.

The pat, pat of Satuma's sandals in the passage aroused Tony from his swift meditations.   Prince Hohenhoff brushed past him at the coolie's invitation to enter, ignoring with Teutonic pride the presence of the little detective in the doorway.

Tony felt that his chances of promotion were not to be lightly assailed. Signalling to one of the detectives, he followed on the Prince's footsteps like one caressing each moment of his life. He knew that the man who had seared the brain and nerves of his comrade Renwick would stop at nothing when his precious liberty was threatened.

The atmosphere of the house seemed charged with the odour of some peculiar mineral substance. Satuma pointed to an open door at the pasage end, and salaamed like a spring-fitted image as both men stepped inside.

A single carbon illumined the apartment, and to Hackett's quick-shifting eyes the place appeared empty. A moment's pause gave breadth to his vision. The face of a small, elfish man was regarding them intently — a nerve-shrunken face with glowing eyes and pale lips. Prince Hohenhoff bowed slightly in Tsarka's direction, the envelope held firmly in his right hand.

Doctor Tsarka's elf-like figure straightened on the instant. Then his eyes flashed over the Prince's tall figure to the round, smiling face of the detective near the door. Something in Tony's attitude aroused his instant wrath.

"My house appears to be at the mercy of every curiosity monger," he declared bitterly. "What is your business, sir?"

Prince Hohenhoff interposed. "I permitted this gentleman to follow me in here," he said with a glance at Tony, "because I am anxious to hear you refute his ill-timed accusations."

He placed the letter in Tsarka's hand and turned slowly toward the door. Tony accepted the gleam in his eyes as a challenge to immediate action.

Prince Hohenhoff spoke again as one who desired to make clear his position in the transaction.

"I came here at the desire of Madame Beatrice Messonier. She appealed to me for protection against the unauthorized people who spy upon her movements. She declares that her correspondence has been tampered with, her telephone communication interrupted, so that she is compelled to rely upon the generosity of her influential patients to carry on her medical labours." The Prince spoke with heat, while the young blood stayed scarlet about his cheeks and throat.

"I do not know if you are aware of these

persecutions," he added with a gesture in Tony's direction.

The little detective shrugged good-humouredly. He was certain now this inexperienced young man had fallen a victim to the charms of his fair physician, and was permitting himself to be drawn unwittingly into an extremely difficult situation. By some strange means (it may have been through the agency of the coolie doorkeeper) Tsarka appeared to have become cognizant of his visitor's high rank. A smile threatened to break the hard lines of the Jap doctor's mouth.

"We have suffered the bitterest persecutions since coming to England," he began in his caressing tones. "On every side we have met opposition and tyranny. This man," he pointed sorrowfully toward the smiling Hackett, "is one of a legion who daily harass Madame Messonier and myself. They impute to us the most hideous motives. I therefore beg that you will not listen to this fellow's impudent ramblings."

Tony flinched at the words; his shoulders stiffened. It was not the first time in life that he had experienced the whips of scorn when confronted by an outwitted criminal.

In the present case his feelings were soothed by the knowledge that he had run to earth a man who had baffled the united wits of Scotland Yard. He addressed Tsarka across the table.

"A warrant has been issued for your arrest, Doctor Tsarka. I will have it read aloud if you choose. In any case you must accompany an officer of the law to the nearest police station, where a charge of conspiring to swindle the Duchess of Marister and Prince Hohenhoff will be preferred against you."

Prince Hohenhoff stared with round eyes at the little detective. "Gott, . . . you are mad!" he almost shouted. "I have not charged Doctor Tsarka with anything!"

"I am very sorry," Tony spoke with a humorous gleam in his brown eye. "This gentleman" — he nodded briefly to the stiff-lipped Japanese doctor — "this gentleman arranged a certain little studio comedy when your Highness, in company with several other distinguished ladies and gentlemen, received a baptism of radium molecules which caused you some pain and inconvenience."

Doctor Tsarka laughed outright, yet Tony observed that his fingers trembled as he laughed. Prince Hohenhoff glared at the immobile Hackett. Then his eyes softened strangely.

"Do you implicate Madame Messonier in this fraud?" he demanded with a sudden show of interest. "Surely you are presuming too much!"

Tony's answer was emphatic and conciliatory. "I must beg your Highness to have patience with me," he averred. "In civilized countries it is the duty of kings and princes to uphold the dignity of the law. I make no charge against Madame Beatrice Messonier. My business lies with Doctor Tsarka."

Prince Hohenhoff bowed with unaffected humility of manner. Something in Tony's outspoken words quieted his rising anger.

"I know nothing of Doctor Tsarka," he volunteered after a brief pause. "It is Madame Messonier's interests I feel bound to protect. . . . She has suffered intensely. She has dedicated her life to the alleviation of suffering in others. I myself am a living witness to her skill and power!" he cried with something like passion in his voice. "Rest assured that any attempt to persecute

or annoy her will be swiftly resented by myself and the Duchess of Marister.''

He turned sharply with a slight bow in
Tsarka's direction, and was about to retire.

The little nerve specialist had remained
quiescent under Tony's scathing allegations,
hoping each moment that his royal visitor
would depart, leaving him free to deal with
the unwelcome intruder. With the Duchess
of Marister's cheque for five thousand guineas
in his pocket he hoped, even at the last
extremity, to obtain bail if Hackett insisted
upon his accompanying him to a police
station.

The Prince's entry upon the scene was,
after all, an unexpected bit of fortune which
might stand him in good stead. The situation bristled with points. But through the
almost kaleidoscopic changes of fortune he
saw very clearly that his beautiful child
genius, Beatrice Messonier, had gained the
heart of an emperor's son.

The thought passed, leaving him cold and
miserable. With the shadow of an English
gaol looming so close, he felt her slipping,
slipping from his withered hands into the
immensity of other worlds.

Prince Hohenhoff had gained the passage; six paces would have taken him to the door. A voice reached him from one of the overhead rooms, a voice he had heard in the Piccadilly studio when the radium-poisoned stereoscope had struck its blinding rays into his brain. The voice was singing a Japanese song of triumph, a song that touched his marrow like naked steel.

He halted with his gloved fist on the door, head thrown back, his teeth set. The song continued and was accompanied by the tramp, tramp of impatient feet. The footsteps crossed the room above and then reached the stair-head. Ten seconds later the head and shoulders of Soto Inouyiti appeared above the banister. He came quickly without a glance to right or left. In his arms he carried a large canvas, which caught the light as he turned into the study, revealing tawny splashes of colour wherein a human face looked out upon the world — the face and head of a dying Japanese boy.

In the study Soto raised the canvas so that the light illumined his incomparable brushwork. He flaunted it before the stiff-limbed Tsarka in triumphant mockery.

"Look, Teroni, at the crucifixion of Soto Inouyiti!" To and fro he waved the picture in the frenzied delight of his achievement. "Salaam, Teroni, for here is the pure light that never shone in your laboratory fires. Put away your radium bulbs and look upon my work!"

He danced across the study, his flamboyant necktie streaming wildly as he danced. In that moment the Jap doctor consigned him to the liquid Gehenna reserved for the impenitent child-slayer.

Inouyiti's loud laughter ended abruptly. A shadow slanted between him and the light. He looked up and stared at the big, blond figure of Prince Hohenhoff, and the canvas slithered from his grasp to the floor.

A soft whistle from Tony brought a detective in from the passage. At a nod he slipped a pair of handcuffs over the young artist's wrists and bundled him carefully into a far corner of the study. Hackett was impressed by the sudden fire in Tsarka's eye.

Prince Hohenhoff gestured approvingly in the detective's direction. "You have done well," he said, "to arrest that little monster. It was he who caused the trouble in the studio.

Gott in Himmel!"   He paused to glance at the quailing Japanese doctor.   "Do you now deny your part in the infernal studio crime?"

Tsarka pointed to the trembling Inouyiti with something of pity in his gesture.

"That boy is suffering from an incurable mental disease.   I must also remind you," he added with a frigid bow, "that this house is used as a private hospital.   Do you hold a physician responsible for the sins of his patients?" he asked quietly.   "Must I answer for the insane conduct of the people who come to me for treatment?"

Prince Hohenhoff shrugged.   "The circumstances are very curious," he admitted thoughtfully.   Then, stooping, he picked up Inouyiti's canvas from the study floor and raised it to the light.

It was the head of a Japanese youth done in oils.   At a glance Prince Hohenhoff, himself a connoisseur of the highest order, detected in the masterly technique and composition the rarest expression of a healthy-minded genius.   He gazed at the picture for what seemed, to the waiting detective, an interminable period.   Then, without lowering the canvas from the light, he spoke in an unchanged voice to the Japanese doctor.

"Did that boy," nodding to Inouyiti, "paint this head?"

"I presume so. Most of his pictures are horrible."

"Are lunatics capable of the highest form of art, such as this?"

"Undoubtedly!" Tsarka responded with a laugh. "If you do not believe me go into the National Gallery. Soto Inouyiti is a morbid degenerate. I am no more responsible for his attack on the Duchess and yourself than I am for the production of that!"

He pointed to the picture with an affectation of scorn that caused the boy artist to glare at him in fierce surprise.

"Was it my lunacy that arranged the poisoned stereoscope, Teroni?" Inouyiti demanded. "Tell this gentleman how you and Horubu drove me to the crime . . . with threats and beatings. Tell him how you drugged me when I came to you from Japan so that you and that fiend Horubu could steal the money I earned by my brush! If I go to prison, I pray that you go with me!"

Tony made a step toward the door, but halted smartly at a glance from Prince Hohenhoff.

"One moment before you call in your men. I want to ask Doctor Tsarka a question."

"Your Highness may put any question to both prisoners," Tony promptly answered.

"It is this," Prince Hohenhoff went on, his whole frame pulsating with an insupportable dread. "Does Beatrice Messonier know the whole truth of this infamous conspiracy to supply her with a host of wealthy clients?"

Tsarka's answer was short and convincing. "She would hardly have sent your Highness to me if she had believed the story of that mad fool Inouyiti!"

Prince Hohenhoff bowed to the sullen-browed Tsarka, and with a nod to Hackett passed into the street.

Tony's assistants entered the house the moment the red-panelled car swung out of the street. Doctor Tsarka gestured somewhat wearily at their sudden entry.

"I have another patient in this house," he said dully. "He is a Japanese army surgeon; he received terrible injuries while experimenting with some of his mineral compounds in the laboratory."

Hackett promised that a couple of trained nurses should take charge of the house until further notice.   A waiting taxicab answered the detective's call, and with Inouyiti and Tsarka beside him the party were soon en route to the nearest police station.

CHAPTER XX

IT WAS admitted in court circles that young Prince Hohenhoff had fallen a victim to the charms of Beatrice Messonier. At the German Legation it was known that his Highness had cancelled all diplomatic engagements for the coming year, and that for the present he had refused definitely to return to Berlin.

Certain sections of the Continental press seized upon the information and rendered it in various guises to an unbelieving public. A prince of the house of Hapsburg was about to enter into the bonds of matrimony with a nameless charlatan, who had, by some mysterious means, achieved a succession of brilliant cures at her now famous Institute!

The unexpected arrest of Doctor Tsarka and Inouyiti came as a thunderclap on the heels of the story. Madame Messonier was to be implicated in the series of radium frauds which had recently startled Europe and America! How would Prince Hohenhoff escape from the network of scandal into which he had been trapped!

Huntingdon Street swarmed with plain-clothes police, yet the beautiful "charlatan," who had saved the Duchess of Marister and Prince Hohenhoff from the destroying effects of Tsarka's radium, remained at liberty.

The reason was not far to seek. Scotland Yard failed at the last moment to produce evidence, presumptive or otherwise, to establish a charge against Gifford Renwick. A sympathetic jury refused to see why a young detective should not accept the only existing means of saving himself from blindness. Gifford's counsel pointed out with passionate emphasis how the young investigator had been trapped in the nerve specialist's laboratory, and rendered helpless by the deadly radium sponge. Would any living creature, the counsel urged, refuse medical treatment at such a time, even though that help were proffered by a member of a notorious radium clique?

In vain did the prosecuting attorney seek to show how Gifford had sought to temporize with the Japanese band of swindlers. For beyond the fact that he had accepted Pepio's cheque, nothing of a specific nature could be charged against him.

After a brief consultation, the jury returned with a verdict of "Not proven," and Gifford left the court carrying with him the sympathy of judge and public alike.

The case against Doctor Tsarka and Soto Inouyiti proceeded slowly enough. Horubu was discovered in the laboratory suffering from terrible burns. The sullen-browed ex-soldier refused all information about himself or the cause of his accident. He admitted, however, that he had driven a heavy motor-car into a crowd of people who had tried to bar his progress. Tsarka, he insisted to the last, was in no way connected with the affair. The boy artist's presence in the car was the result of intimidation. Inouyiti had been compelled to accompany him on his terrible mission only after the most violent persuasions.

The investigation into the studio outrage presented its comedy aspect to the astonished world. The evidence of the "Spotted Baron" merely accentuated the farcical side of an otherwise tragic conspiracy.

The final attitude of Prince Hohenhoff

toward Inouyiti was entirely sympathetic. Indeed, when the story of the unhappy boy artist became known, public opinion was in favour of his instant acquittal. In the dock Teroni Tsarka remained cynically obdurate under the castigating remarks of the prosecuting counsel. He was compelled to admit that he had founded the Messonier Institute, a fact which gained him a degree of favour in view of the remarkable cures which were now being daily recorded from its operating rooms.

Madame Messonier had already increased her hospital staff to meet the needs of the wealthy patients who now journeyed from all parts of Europe to undergo her famous course of radio-magnetics. All through Tsarka's trying cross-examination not a single statement was elicited that might cast the faintest slur upon the genuineness of her science and knowledge.

Gifford's evidence decided the case for the International Bureau, and exhibited with pitiless truth and judgment the real Teroni Tsarka who had sought to inflict insufferable pain and terror upon certain members of society.

Admissions of his own tardiness in arresting Horubu and Doctor Tsarka were also forthcoming, together with the real cause of his indecision.   Common law, if not always logical, is sometimes human, and Gifford Renwick received a measure of congratulation from the presiding judge for the ignominious part he had chosen to play rather than jeopardize the lives of several innocent people.

Strangely enough Gifford bore no ill-will toward the little Japanese doctor who had practically destroyed his career.   It had been an affair of wits between them, and neither had won.

The trial terminated after many days — days wherein counsel badgered counsel and personal insults blew thick as leaves about the heads of the contending parties.   One circumstance stayed clear in the minds of the jury — that Beatrice Messonier had completed her cures in all innocence of Tsarka's motives.   She was attended throughout the trial by the Duchess of Marister and Prince Hohenhoff.   The childlike simplicity of her evidence, together with the story of her bitter struggles in the past, won her the instant sympathy of the court.

Doctor Tsarka received two years' imprisonment. Inouyiti escaped with a severe lecture from the judge on the folly of borrowing money from criminal adventurers. At the instigation of the court Paul Isaacson was compelled to disgorge the *cache* of radium which he had bargained to purchase from Horubu. It was eventually returned to Prof. Eugene Moritz, its rightful owner.

Gifford emerged from the close-packed court as one treading the paths of failure and defeat. It was in his mind to begin life again in the United States as a clerk or ranchman. He still had a few pounds to his credit in the Twickenham bank. His mother would go with him and help him to live down the bitter experiences of the past.

He turned to cross the road and discovered a liveried footman hastening from the courthouse in his direction.

"I beg your pardon, Mr. Renwick," the fellow panted. "Her Grace would be glad to see you for a few minutes."

Gifford was inclined to laugh at so unusual a request, until he recalled the distinguished lady with the kindly eyes and gray hair who had followed his evidence with such keen interest. Bracing himself instinctively, he accompanied the footman to a blue-panelled landaulette that stood some distance from the court-house.

He was concious of a woman's eyes scanning him closely from the interior of the elegant equipage, of a jewelled fan swinging to and fro among the cushions.

The Duchess of Marister leaned forward at his approach. "I am very pleased to meet you, Mr. Renwick," she declared in her pleasant voice. "Your conduct throughout this miserable investigation has been heroic."

Gifford flushed under his sun-tan, and responded in terms which merely heightened her admiration for his modesty and restraint.

"Do you think," she went on enthusiastically, "that the men who rush to the cannon's mouth are the only heroes? The truest heroism is that which forces men to sit still in the presence of real danger. What would have happened to me or Prince Hohenhoff if you had arrested Madame Messonier in your eagerness to acquire a little professional notoriety?"

Gifford was silent.

The Duchess tapped his fingers with her jewelled fan. "Shall I tell you what would

have happened if Tsarka and madame had
been arrested between the seventh and ninth
of October?"

"It is possible that your Grace would have
lost the use of your sight. At that period,
October the seventh, I was not certain how
far Dr. Teroni Tsarka's influence extended
over the Radium Institute. I thought it
better to wait," he said quietly.

"And in doing so sacrificed your professional honour and reputation!" she vouchsafed. "I know," she continued, glancing
at his reddening cheeks, "the answer I should
earn if I were to offer you monetary compensation."

Gifford flinched and bent his head.

"Well, I shall not presume," she laughed,
"but there is no earthly reason why a Marister
should not feel grateful, Mr. Renwick. And
I trust that we may know each other better
in future."

It was a stereotyped little compliment,
but Gifford detected a genuine warmth
behind her words. As he turned to take
his leave he caught the shadow of a profile
in the far corner of the landaulette. The hot
blood vaulted instantly to his cheeks.

"Miss Cranstone!" he almost cried out.

The Duchess of Marister laughed heartily.

"Another of your silent admirers, Mr. Renwick! Won't you shake hands?"

The beautiful face of the young comedy actress peeped shyly over the Duchess' shoulder; her gloved hand sought his instinctively.

It was with difficulty that Violet had restrained herself with Gifford standing so near. She had not forgotten his almost Quixotic bearing during the trying moments when the Scotland Yard men were clamouring at the doors of the operating theatre.

"I, too, have to thank you, Mr. Renwick," she declared, "for my very existence when that horrid Tsarka threatened to ruin us with his fees!"

"Mine has gone to build a new wing in the Messonier Institute!" the Duchess admitted. "Beatrice would not have it otherwise. The cheque was very promptly returned to me by a Mr. Hackett."

It was evident to Gifford that Miss Cranstone's personality had attracted the Duchess of Marister. He learned afterward that their acquaintance had begun within Beatrice Messonier's consulting rooms when the terror of blindness hung over them both. The Duchess refused to take leave until he had promised to visit her at "Cortillion," her country seat in Herts.

"We are going to recuperate," she declared. "We are going to motor and eat with the county families. And afterward —— " She glanced swiftly at Miss Cranstone.

"To work," the young actress responded. "I have an offer to begin at the Comedy Theatre next month at the modest salary of £200 a week!"

"Those dreadful newspapers," the Duchess exclaimed, patting the young girl's cheek, "have been referring to my little protégée as the heroine of the Big Radium Mystery. London is talking of nothing but Violet Cranstone and her fearful experiences in the Japanese chamber of horrors. Good-by, Mr. Renwick. Come and see Miss Cranstone at 'Cortillion.'"

Gifford left them, feeling more of a failure than ever. The radium gods had bestowed favours on several actors in the recent drama. Tony Hackett had strengthened his position at the International Inquiry Bureau with additional increments to his salary. Beatrice

Messonier was reaping a harvest of fees from her increasing list of patients, while Violet Cranstone's popularity had been considerably enhanced by the strange story of her experience in the radium-poisoned atelier.

For himself there remained the gratitude of an aristocratic lady whose emotions guided her into the most extravagant acts of kindness. He could not help a thrill of joy at the thought of Violet Cranstone's escape from blindness. The opportunity of meeting her again dispelled the gray films of depression which threatened to cloud his mind.

Returning to his home at Twickenham, Gifford received his final surprise the following morning. It was a letter from Hardinge K. Hardinge, the New York millionaire, who had suffered only slightly from Inouyiti's shower of radium molecules. The letter was characteristic of the man:

DEAR MR. RENWICK: Prince Hohenhoff was good enough to mention your name to me. Of course, I was present at the Tsarka trial, and I am one of the many who appreciated your efforts to check what might have been a very pitiable tragedy. If you could spare an hour to dine with me this evening, at the American Club, in Piccadilly, I have it in my hands to assign you a position of trust which would prove beneficial to us both.

Gifford joyfully accepted the invitation, and discovered that the "assignment" was really a position of trust in a firm of financiers over which Mr. Hardinge held a controlling influence. A week after his appointment he was able to pay a short visit to "Cortillion," where Violet Cranstone was preparing for her coming season at the Comedy Theatre.

The Duchess of Marister already regarded Gifford and Violet as her especial protégés. It needed small efforts on her part, however, to bring them constantly together during his brief stay at "Cortillion." Her Grace lost no time in discovering that Gifford was the son of a very distinguished Indian army captain who had rendered inestimable service to her brother during the Sepoy mutiny. In the late September, when the Duchess again brought the young people together at her house, it looked as though the radium gods were bent on filling their lives with a burning joy known only to those who have suffered the pangs of their white-shafted wrath.

Violet had ended her brilliantly successful season at the Comedy Theatre feeling just a trifle weary of the glitter and stress of her

surroundings. Her manager was thunder-
struck by her refusal to renew her contract
at a salary which seemed sufficiently muni-
ficent to tempt a Bernhardt.

Later, when his eye fell upon a cross-headed
announcement in a fashionable evening journal, he cast the paper from him in genuine
anger.

"She's going to marry a fellow named
Renwick," he declared to his secretary. "And
the Duchess of Marister worked like a jack-
tar to make her first season a success. Deuce
take it! I thought we had the West End
society crowd tied to our box office!"

He might have added that the Duchess had
worked with equal enthusiasm to secure
the life-long engagement of two young people
whose love for each other was more enduring
than the limelight and tinsel of a fashionable
comedy theatre.

CONCLUSION

THE night had flung a veil of mist across the river where the swart barges lay huddled under the bridge-span. Two figures stole toward one of the recesses, where the lamp-glow revealed the tear-swollen features of Pepio Tsarka. Her hand rested lightly on Soto Inouyiti's arm as the young artist stared dreamfully at the illumined reflections below. Here and there a panting launch cast a scarlet flare over the face of the river, while in the distance the City lamps wove miracles of colour and shade through the indriving fog.

Inouyiti did not address the weeping Japanese girl until his eye had drunk its fill of London's inimitable nightpiece. Sighing very softly, he peered down at the tiny gloved hand resting against his sleeve. The lights of the river seemed to pinch his eyes.

"There is no colour like the colour of Japan, Pepio. My heart cries for the temple shadows and the red eaves of our old pagodas. Where are the wine-red poppies of my dear Nagasaki, the lanterns that bloomed at night under the Dragon archway?"

Pepio leaned over the bridge parapet, and her childish sobbing stirred to flame the dozing fires in Soto's eyes. Her breath quickened as he stooped near her.

"I have been very unhappy, too, Pepio, because a woman of another race looked at me with cold eyes and lips. Perhaps it is well that kind should mate with kind, the fair with the fair. Shall we, Pepio, go back to our lilies and chrysanthemums? Shall we return to Nippon to paint in black and vermillion the tones of our temples and skies?"

"Ohe, ata sotana!"

"Then we will return and wait for your father, my Pepio. Come, come to me, my dear, and our children shall play and sing near the red shrines where our people lie. Come, Pepio."

The bridge lamp cast a beam in Pepio's eye as she raised her face to the artist's lips.

THE END

www.ingramcontent.com/pod-product-compliance
Lightning Source LLC
Chambersburg PA
CBHW032228010726
47494CB00002B/393